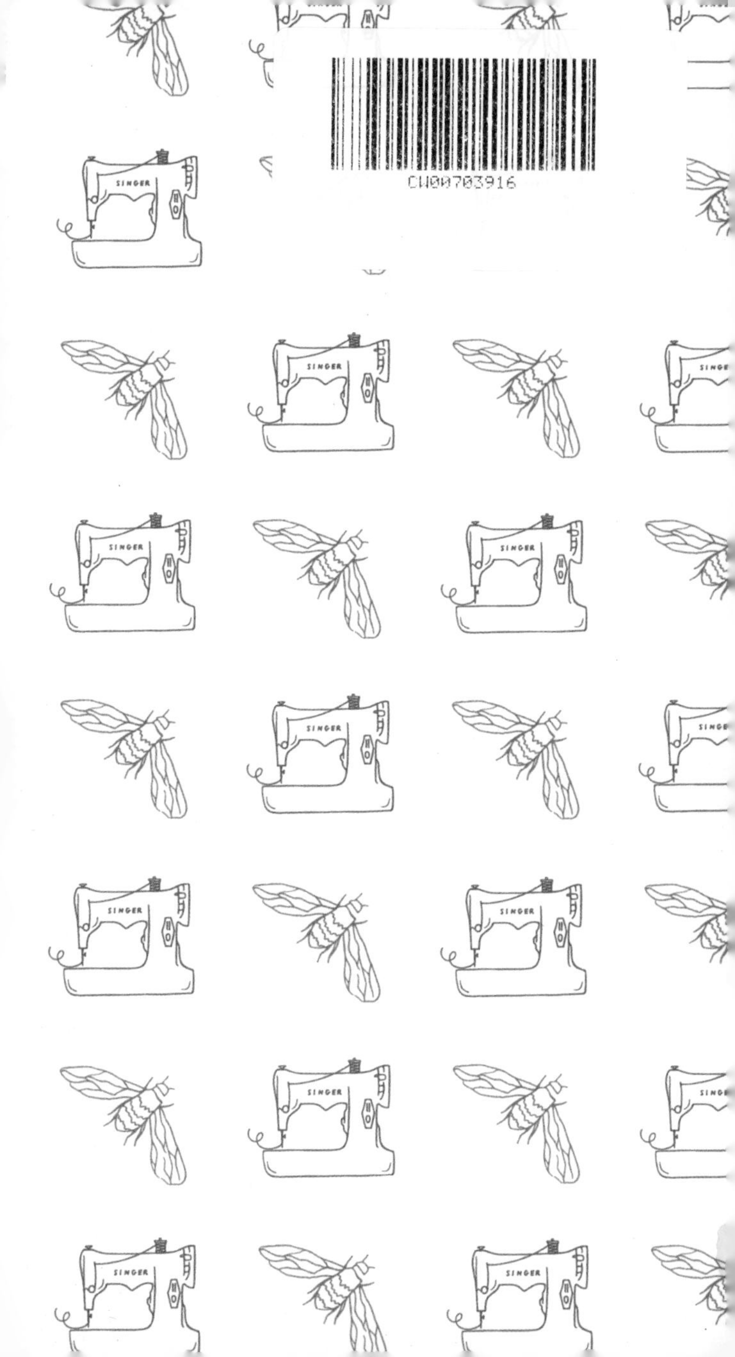
CW00703916
SINGER

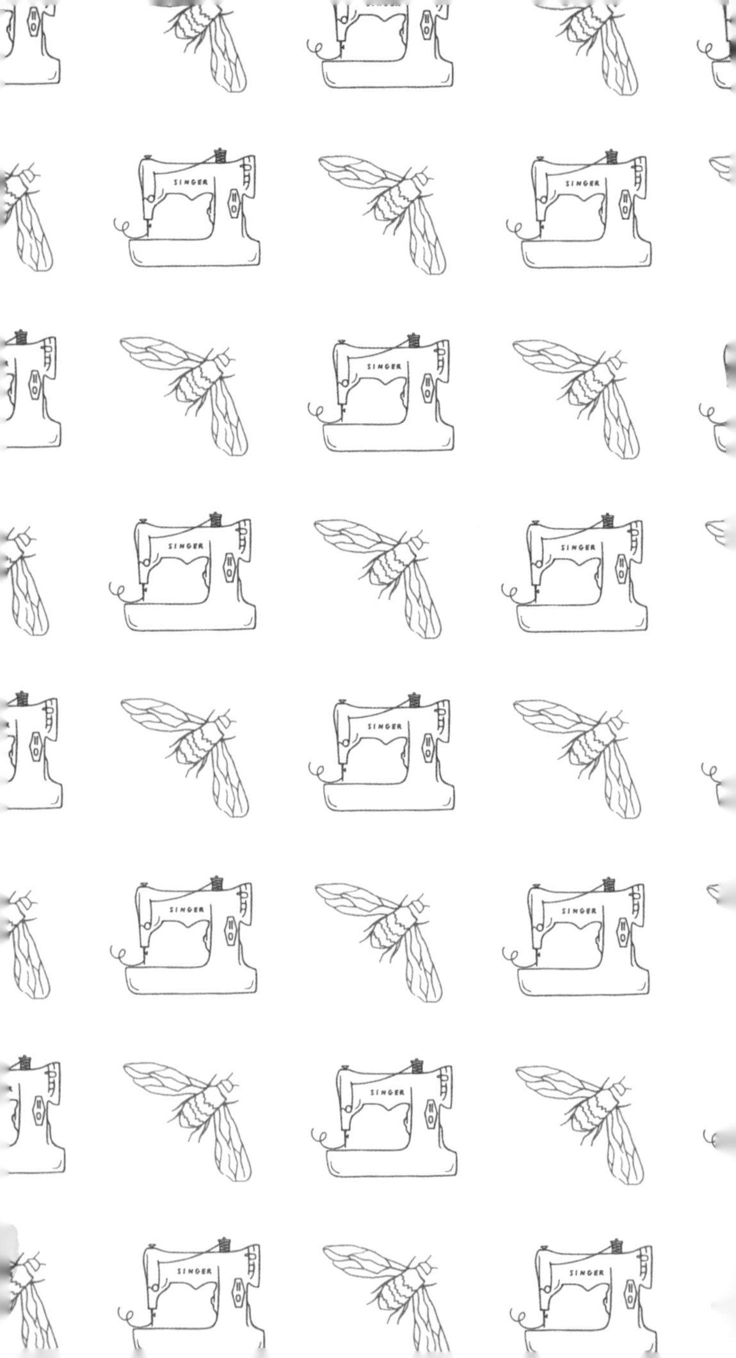
SINGER
SINGER
SINGER
SINGER
SINGER
SINGER
SINGER
SINGER
SINGER
SINGER
SINGER

The Bras

and the

Bees

The
Extraordinary Life
of BJ Sherriff

FA Notley

First published in Great Britain in 2019 by Scryfa

ISBN: 978-1-9997598-3-4

British Library Cataloguing in Publication Data; a catalogue
record for this book is available from the British Library
Produced in the UK by BluemoonPrint

To Pat – together we walked as one.
Brian Sherriff

Brian Sherriff
in his days as a square-dance caller

Foreword

If you're a beekeeper, you'll be well familiar with Sherriff products, said to be the Rolls-Royce of beesuits. Under the direction of the company's founder Brian Sherriff, they're recognised and appreciated internationally in their distinctive pastel colours. I've worn one for years. It's red, as that's apparently the colour that bees can't make out. When I bought it, I calculated that if they can't see you, they can't sting you.

You might be surprised to learn then, that Brian has spent most of his life in ladies' underwear. I know, I was shocked as well. It turns out that the master of the modern bee suit (complete with elasticated cuffs, velcro fastenings, the twin-zip system and indispensable thumb loop) is an expert in the manufacture of corsets and, um, brassieres. It was the family business in which Brian grew up.

So how did he progress from lingerie to bee hoods? Well, that's the story Felicity Notley is about to tell you, along with tales of Brian's adventures abroad, back when travelling to Europe involved considerably more than just hopping on a cheap flight.

You'll also learn about his connection to the play *Journey's End*, how he became at one point 'Sheriff Bryan' leader of a square dance posse, and the fabulous invention he used to demonstrate his company's prowess: the Bra-kerchief. Yes, that is what you think it is. I don't know whether you could blow your nose on it.

Nowadays BJ Sherriff sell all sorts of bee-related items such as gauntlets, hive tools, ties and cufflinks – but not, disappointingly (given the family history), ladies' undergarments. Well, not yet. I may just have given them an idea.

Even if you're not a bee-keeper, I'm sure you'll find the story of Brian's life engaging, harking as it does back to simpler, slower times.

Bill Turnbull

Contents

Introduction

To bee-keepers across the world, BJ Sherriff is known for his bespoke beekeeping clothing, which features a distinctive sheriff's star. To those who've had the good fortune to meet him, it's his calm and cheerful personality that is unforgettable.

With Brian I have been spoilt. At our weekly meetings for the preparation of this book, he outshone me every time, due to the extent and thoroughness of his 'homework'. He had diaries, photograph albums, posters from his square-dancing days, leather wrist gauntlets worn by his aunt in Guyana, a daguerreotype photograph, a suitcase full of antique corsets and – most intriguingly of all – several original examples of his finest invention, The Bra-kerchief.

This book tells the story of a man who inherited a business, lost it, started from scratch and created one of the most successful beekeeping clothing brands ever. Brought up to the family business of corsetry, he went on to run his own bra factory in Camborne, Cornwall in the south west of England, before becoming a pioneer in beekeeping clothing. BJ Sherriff beesuits are still made in Cornwall and Brian visits his sewing-machinists once a week to exchange pre-cut fabric for finished garments. These are then parcelled up and distributed across the world.

One day when I go in to interview Brian, to talk to him about his life, I have a cough sweet in my mouth. I'm preoccupied with establishing the correct spelling of his grandmother's name and am surprised when he says, rather sternly: 'You're not meant to crunch on them. You're meant to let them dissolve slowly.'

'You're right,' I concede. I look across at him. His pale blue eyes are twinkling. 'You're making me want one now,' he says.

I suspect that Brian, at ninety years of age, is not much different from Brian at nineteen. It's impossible to spend any time with him and not be in a good mood.

FA Notley
Falmouth, 2018

1

Bee Man

It was once Brian's dream to join the circus – this photograph was taken by Brian in 1948

Bee Man

It is late summer. The year is 1968. Brian Sherriff is driving back from Dartmoor to Cornwall with forty beehives on his trailer. But something's not right. The trailer is keeling off to one side. A flat tyre. He clambers out, checks in the back of the car for a spare wheel. The light is fading but he could do this with his eyes shut. He's been messing around with cars all his life. He fits the wheel to the trailer and continues on his way.

When the spare tyre also bursts just minutes later, his options are limited. It's dusk. He's on a long road miles from anywhere. He sets off on foot, looking for the nearest house. When he finds it, he asks to use a telephone and roadside assistance is not long in coming. The trailer is winched onto a low loader. Brian gives detailed directions of how to find his house and sets off once again, down the narrow twisty roads that will lead him home. The trailer, he assumes, and the beehives rich with heather honey, are right behind him.

At home, however, time passes. Night falls and still there is no sign of the bees. Brian makes a telephone call. He wonders if the trailer has got lost. Instead he's told that, due to the late hour, the trailer has been put in a warehouse overnight. It will be delivered in a few days' time.

'Is the warehouse heated?' Brian asks.

'Yes sir.'

'There are forty beehives on that trailer,' Brian starts to explain, trying not to succumb to rising panic. 'Forty beehives with sixty thousand bees in each – that's two million, four hundred thousand bees. And if the hives get warm, the bees will come out...'

The trailer is returned to him that very night. The bees arrive shortly after midnight in a convoy of flashing lights, one van in front and one behind, as befits royalty.

The next day Brian lifts the lid off the first beehive, dismantling it one section at a time, to see how much honey has accumulated. More than he expected.

Brian was never meant to be a bee man though. His career was mapped out for him long before he was born. Though he dreamt briefly of running away to join the circus, that was never really an option. His family's past had determined his future.

He knows the story well – how once, long ago, his grandfather bought a corset factory from a Mr Langridge in Bristol. And he's familiar with a scene that played out decades before his birth: the move from Temple Street to Church Road. He can picture it almost as if he'd been there himself: the young machinists in their long skirts, lifting up their Singer sewing-machines, boarding the tram and making a solemn procession to the new factory premises.

Corsetry was what Brian was born to do and he's been working with corsets and, more recently, bras ever since he was old enough to work. But of late something's changed. Increasingly, orders which would have come to him have started to go abroad. His main customers, instead of stocking bras made in Cornwall, have been ordering them from overseas. It's a question of market forces. It seems no time at all since he was putting advertisements in the paper to recruit more machinists. Soon, it seems, those same papers will carry headlines of imminent redundancies.

Brian peers into the hive; the heavy bee-keeper's hat he's wearing slips forward so that the veil lies flat against the back of his neck. Almost at once a bee takes advantage of the accessible skin and stings him. A sharp needle in the back of the neck, that strange spreading numbness he's so familiar with.

That night at dinner with his wife Pat the idea is already half formed.

'What's the use of beekeeping clothing if it doesn't protect you from bees?' he says. 'It's silly getting stung. We could do better.'

And later that week at the factory, Pat gathers together the materials normally used for making bras: boning, net, poly-cotton. She even snaffles a bolt of fabric intended for swimming costume gussets. She sets about designing an improved bee-keeper's veil. What she creates will change the face of beekeeping forever.

2

The Beginning

The wedding of Brian's parents, Jack and Joan

The Beginning

Brian's life began with an error. He was born in Bristol, just a mile from the Clifton Suspension Bridge in a maternity home that no longer exists. His mother Joan lovingly recorded the date as 24 May 1929 in a book entitled *Baby Days*. His birth certificate, however, states that he was born in 1928. To this day, Brian is not entirely sure which is correct. A curious beginning to an extraordinary life.

Although not actually born with a silver spoon in his mouth, Brian was at least very well provided for and by the time he was baptised, this oversight had been corrected, as he was presented with not one, but two silver spoons at his Christening, one of them with a crest. All of this was noted in *Baby Days*, a keepsake journal with questions and space left for a mother to fill in fond details. Brian still has it. It has a pale blue cover, embossed with the image of a young boy in a smock sitting at the foot of a sundial. The image provides the perfect evocation of leisure, pleasure and the passage of time. Joan's handwriting is surprisingly modern; her confidently rounded letters owe nothing to the spidery copper-plate of the previous era.

The gifts that welcomed Brian into the world were lavish and very much of their time. He was treated to nine matinée coats (seven of wool, one of voile, one of silk), four pairs of woollen leggings, nighties (apparently not just for girls), two voile frocks (likewise), a silver rattle on a mother-of-pearl ring, various pieces of china, a pillow and two pillow cases, a blue silk eiderdown, a woollen shawl, a small bathing chair, two bibs, one pair of woollen gloves, two baby baskets, silk roses and a Marmet pram and pram cover.

Baby Days is punctuated with advertisements and one of these features a Marmet pram. A black and white illustration depicts a nurse in cap and apron taking Baby out for a ride, while Grandpa looks on in top hat, striped trousers and spats, inspecting the pram through a monocle. At the back of the book are tear-out postcards for free samples of various items. The most tempting of these was from Gibbs, who offered a free copy of *The Ivory Castle Fairy Book* along with trial packets of various toiletries for ladies or gentlemen.

With such an auspicious start, it is not surprising that Brian exceeded the weights listed as 'normal' in the baby book, was able to say 'Golly golly' at eight months and learnt to 'creep' (the word used at the time for 'crawling') by March the following year.

When Brian's father came home from work, he would fill the house with music. He had wired up the whole building and fitted loudspeakers in every room, with the effect that when he listened to Henry Hall's dance band music in one room, it could be heard throughout the house. When asked what his mother thought about this, Brian says: 'I don't know. Perhaps she was never asked.'

Brian's mother's real name was Dorothy, but she was always known as Joan. She had married Brian's father, Jack, on 10 September 1925 at St Alban's Church, Westbury Park, Bristol. A newspaper cutting described the ceremony: 'The bride was given away by her father and looked exceedingly nice in a gown of white charmeuse and lace and a train, also of charmeuse, caught on the shoulders with sprigs of orange blossom.' In the official group photograph, Joan has her hand tucked into the crook of Jack's arm. Her expression is dreamy and he looks very pleased with himself.

Jack and Joan spent their honeymoon on Jersey. The honeymoon snaps can be found in an album shuffled with subsequent holiday photographs and even include images of Brian as a baby, as if he had always been a part of the family. In fact, he did not appear on the scene until two and a half years later, if his birth certificate is to be believed.

One photograph shows Joan in the grounds of the St Aubin's Bay Hotel on Jersey. She is dressed in typical 1920s fashion, with bobbed hair and a voluminous drop-waisted dress. In a second photograph she is perched in the sidecar of a motorbike wearing a scarf, leather flying cap and goggles. In a third she has a headscarf wound round her head and the caption, written by Jack, reads: 'The Gipsy.' The album is packed with West Country holidays, beach cottages, picnics and tents.

An idyllic life, but there was more to Joan than met the eye. This is the woman who would later give her teenage son a copy of *Naked and Unashamed*, causing him to receive his first ever caning when it was discovered in his desk at school, the same woman who would adopt the new fashion of wearing slacks with characteristic elegance and who would, thanks to her cool head and good common sense, one day save her husband's life. But all that was yet to come.

Jack comes across as a serious fellow in the images, a man in control of his emotions, and yet the captions he's added to the photographs demonstrate a wry sense of humour. His boat bore the name PTO (Please Turn Over). He was appropriately dressed for every occasion. For golf, he wore plus fours and long socks with a diamond pattern. In one photograph taken on Exmoor, Jack is sitting half in, half out of a small tent. His legs are bent in front of him and he is clasping his knees. He looks both awkward and stern. In a companion photograph, no doubt taken by Jack as they swapped roles, Joan is the one in the tent. By contrast, she has an insouciant air, seems more a child of nature.

In fact, holidays aside, Joan's early married life might have been a little quiet for her. A keen student of the pianoforte, she moved into a flat with her husband which had no piano and in one set of dark, moody photographs, she appears somewhat swamped by the fixtures and furnishings. It's possible that she may even have been a bit lonely while Jack was out at work. Like many other educated married women, she turned to reading for solace.

In the play *Still Life* by Noel Coward, on which the film *Brief Encounter* is based, it says of the heroine: 'She is reading a Boots library book at which she occasionally smiles.' Joan was one of a certain class of women used to making regular visits to Boots the chemist, whose ministry to the nation's health at that time extended to lending libraries.

Boots libraries were havens of tranquility for women like Joan and provided intellectual stimulation which might otherwise have been missing from their lives. They were normally situated at the back of a Boots pharmacy or on a separate floor altogether. The architecture and décor had been lovingly designed, inspired by the Arts and Craft movement. There were wooden bookshelves, parquet floors, sofas and rugs and window seats. In some Boots libraries there were even stained-glass windows and views out over the town.

Certain novels, such as DH Lawrence's *Sons and Lovers,* had a red label stuck on the inside and were not filed on the shelves but kept under the counter. Joan favoured romantic novels.

Brian's brother, Anthony Bernard, was born in 1931. The wonder surrounding babyhood may have lost some of its shine for his parents by this time. Anthony (known as Tony) did not receive his own baby book but was granted a share in his brother's. Details of his weight at birth, first steps and unique talents were squeezed in alongside those of Brian. However, Tony did have one advantage over his elder brother. His date of birth was recorded correctly.

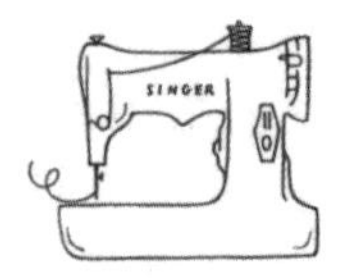
SINGER

3

The Corset Factory

Factory life was conducted to the efficient whirr of some thirty Singer sewing machines

The Corset Factory

Every day while the children played, their father made his way to the corset factory at 248a Church Road, St George, Bristol. He was the director and his working life had its own soundtrack: the efficient whirr of some thirty Singer sewing machines.

Sometimes Brian and Tony were allowed to visit. They loved the mysterious, characterful building, which had once been a dance hall and theatre.

The factory operated on two floors and, as the garments gradually took shape, they made a complete tour of the building. The process started when new bolts of fabric arrived and were taken to the cutting room on the ground floor. Marks were made on the fabric in pencil according to a pattern. To ensure minimum wastage, the placing of the pattern was critical. Next, the fabric had to be carefully folded, so that the knife could cut as many layers as possible in one go.

The man who operated the jig knife, who was known as 'the cutter', was never seen without his felt cap. Brian suspected that this was to cover his bald head. The six-inch blade moved up and down through the material powered by an electric drive wheel under the table.

The pre-cut fabric, known as 'cut work', was then sent upstairs by means of a rope lift to the sewing room, which was filled with the sweet, fresh smell of fabric. The sewing-machinists were all women and girls – some as young as fourteen – and they made up the largest body of employees within the factory. Two sisters, Gertrude and Hilda Pearce, were in charge. Gertrude was the manager of the machinists and Hilda was in charge of quality control. Brian was rather frightened of Gertrude.

The range of garments to be made included front lace corsets, back lace corsets and hookside corsets with hook and eye fastenings. Structure was provided by steel bones, which were inserted into channels made of webbing. The garments had to be made in stages using a variety of different sewing machines.

The sewing machines were placed in

rows on either side of the room. All the machines were connected to a belt that ran from one end of the room to the other. In this way, they all shared the same power supply and did not have individual motors. Wooden troughs were situated next to each sewing-machinist. Once a machinist had completed a piece of work, she placed it in the trough next to her and picked out a new one from the trough behind, so that a production line was created.

Finished garments were taken to quality control where each corset was trimmed with scissors and carefully inspected for faults. If deemed satisfactory, it was then rolled in tissue paper, placed in a box and sent down a chute to the despatch room. There the parcels would be made up by a young man named Ron Catford, ready to be sent out to customers.

Brian and Tony were fascinated by the chute, which seemed just the right size for a small boy. They secretly and desperately wanted to try it out. They had discussed the matter in private and decided that the only way would be to take their chance when the two Miss Pearces were otherwise occupied. So one day, when Jack had gathered his staff around him to discuss some dull adult topic, Tony got into the chute and slid down. At the bottom he was greeted by an amazed Ron. After this successful test run, with only minor injuries in the form of splinters, the chute became irresistible to the two boys.

Brian and Tony developed a particular friendship with the mechanic, Percy Miller. He told them that his workshop was in what had once been the ticket office, when the building had been a dance hall and theatre.

Percy had a bald head, a moustache and one prominent tooth at the front of his mouth, a feature which was known at the time as 'a pickle chaser'. Brian, Tony and Percy had one thing in common: their birthdays all fell on the 24th day of the month. To celebrate the fact, Percy made special badges for all of them, to show that they were members of an exclusive club.

Factory hours were 8am to 5pm, five and a half days a week, until the half day on Saturdays was dropped, giving employees a full weekend off. Talking was permitted but, as each sewing-machinist was paid by piece work, there was a good reason to keep one's mind on the job; any sub-standard stitching would have been noticed by one of the two Miss Pearces and rejected.

Singing was allowed for one hour each morning and the girls sang all the popular songs of the day. The former dance hall had not entirely lost its swing. It was an exciting time, musically speaking, and the influence of Charleston, jazz, big band numbers and ballroom tunes was all-pervasive. On Friday and Saturday evenings most of the machinists went out dancing after work.

Jack's office was situated on the first floor and had windows overlooking the road. A short corridor with a glass roof led from there to the sewing room and the canteen was just below – very convenient for cups of tea. Brian was impressed by everything he saw at the factory, but in particular he admired his father's secretary, Angela Verran. He remembers her glowing ginger hair and the fact that she had her own office.

After lunch every day, Jack was in the habit of retiring to his office and putting his feet up on the low mantlepiece for a short snooze. To a casual observer, it might have seemed as if he did not have a care in the world, but Jack was as aware as everyone else of rumours of an impending war.

4

The Gentleman Bicyclist

Portrait of EJ Sherriff, Brian's grandfather

The Gentleman Bicyclist

Brian's story properly begins two generations before him, with the purchase of a corset factory by his grandfather, Edgar John Sherriff. A scrapbook, meticulously kept by Edgar, provides a great insight into his life and personality. This book came into Brian's keeping when it was entrusted to him by an aunt.

The last time Brian saw his grandfather their ages were three and seventy-six respectively. Edgar was lying in bed and Brian had been called to his bedside for a final goodbye. Brian remembers his white hair and full white moustache.

That same bountiful moustache can be seen on a much younger man in a portrait of Edgar which appeared in *Bicycling News* fifty years earlier. The portrait was pasted onto an opening page of Edgar's scrapbook. It is exactly the kind of illustration you might expect to see in a Sherlock Holmes novel. The young man looking out of the page has dark curly hair with a centre parting, sideburns, a handlebar moustache (appropriately enough) and slightly ragged eyebrows. The lapels of his coat are rounded and he wears a starched collar. His cravat is held neatly in place by a pin. In short, he looks very much the part of a keen gentleman cyclist and it would be easy to imagine him becoming embroiled in a mystery that could only be solved by the master detective.

The scrapbook, a hefty volume with a pale purple cover, is now very fragile. The spine has almost completely disintegrated. By carefully turning the pages, one can see that it contains hundreds of cuttings relating to cycling news and other sporting events. Leafing through the book, certain points of similarity between Brian and his grandfather emerge: a sense of adventure, boundless energy and a slightly obsessive passion for making lists.

In 1879, at the age of twenty-four, Edgar had written to the editor of *Bicycling News*. When his letter was printed, he cut it out of the publication and pasted it into his scrapbook. The letter gives the number of miles he had cycled in the previous year, and even by today's standards it's staggering.

In the month of July alone the total number of miles had been 1,033 and he doesn't scrimp on the details: he had cycled on 16 different days that month and the longest distance cycled in a single day was 105 miles. The total number of miles he'd cycled in the whole year came to 4,032.

It seems that Edgar's enthusiasm paid off: he was officially named as a contributor to *Bicycling News* – and presumably his portrait was commissioned for this reason.

Edgar's call to cyclists is just as appealing today as it was over a century ago. 'A fine frosty morning,' he wrote, 'a clear sky overhead, the frost sparkling on every bough, the fields of dazzling brightness, and with a good hard road under you is just the sort of morning for bicycling.' The word 'bicycling' it seems was always used in full and never shortened to 'cycling'.

In one article he described how his passion was born, and his initial difficulties. He playfully summarised the content of the article in a 'chapter' heading reminiscent of a Henry Fielding novel. 'How I Learnt To Ride A Bicycle: My ambition is aroused... I take lessons... am rather awkward... smash a spring... charge a window... the result... my last lesson... the dismounting... I damage my unmentionables... and sneak home.'

It took him two years to graduate from novice to expert, which might seem slow going, but when one considers that he was probably riding a Penny Farthing, with one wheel the size of a dinner gong and the other the size of a dessert platter, it becomes easier to understand. Penny Farthings were well-known for their propensity to throw the rider forward. In fact, it is probably an indication of Edgar's strength of character that he not only tamed the bicycles of his day, but became an expert in the field, racking up mileages that would impress even a modern amateur rider.

Edgar referred to his bicycle as his 'steel steed' and sometimes even 'the pigskin', the traditional material for making saddles. 'The pigskin was again taken to,' he wrote, as if he were in the grips of an addiction. Perhaps he was.

With so much time spent riding bicycles and writing about his passion, it is hard to imagine how Edgar had time to found a family dynasty. And yet the scrapbook provides evidence of certain developments in Edgar's life.

A document flutters out, not glued in place, merely tucked in between the pages. It's a receipt from a manufacturer in Bristol for items suggestive of domesticity and family life: a bedstead, a mattress, a stair carpet. The receipt has been printed with the merchant's name and address, but the date has not been filled in. It simply bears the pre-printed century '18–', with a space left to fill in the last two digits by hand.

Another receipt follows. This time it is for purchases at The Pinafore Shop and dated June 1897. The articles of clothing listed include a nightdress, frocks, blouses, a cape, buttons, a lounge dress and a dressing jacket. A charge is made for the cleaning and mending of garments. The reckoning comes to three pounds, six shillings and fourpence ha'penny. It seems that Edgar John Sherriff had become a family man.

Plotting a life by means of a scrapbook is of course not the only way. Parallel research by means of official documents confirms that by the time the receipt for The Pinafore Shop was made out, Edgar had been married for seven years. His bride, who boasted the wonderfully Anglo-Saxon name of Bertha Emily Thickbroom, was the daughter of a watch-case maker and eleven years his junior.

The wedding took place on 25 September 1890 in Dulwich, south London, with witnesses present from the bride's side of the family only, a fact which could suggest that the Sherriffs did not approve the match. Sadly, in the months following the wedding, Bertha lost both her parents, her mother dying just a week after the ceremony and her father at the end of the year.

As the receipt suggests, the couple went on to have children. In total Bertha brought six children into the world between the years of 1891 and 1901. Their names were Dorothy, Kathleen, Bernard, Gladys, Phyllis and lastly Jack, the youngest, who would one day be Brian's father.

As the children grew up, their own sporting successes started to elbow their father's achievements out of the way in the scrapbook. Two of Edgar's daughters feature prominently: Kathleen, usually known as Kay, and Gladys. Kay was the winner of the Gloucester County Ladies Championship for swimming, played for Clifton Ladies Lacrosse Club and taught gymnastics and Swedish drill. Clearly she had inherited her father's athleticism. A newspaper cutting reveals that she married Albert Victor Montgomery in 1921 – 'a very useful man at cricket, hockey and tennis' – and the well-matched couple moved to Norfolk Island in the Pacific Ocean. In fact, it was to Kay that Edgar gave the book of cuttings when he grew elderly and it was Kay who later entrusted the scrapbook to Brian.

Gladys, it seems, was quite as impressive as her sister. She moved with her husband to British Guiana (now Guyana), where she was credited with being the first woman to swim the British Guiana River. Her husband, Mr Ashburner, was a plantation overseer and Gladys would ride around the perimeter of the plantation on horseback, wearing leather gauntlets to protect her skin from the spines of cacti. She always had a Colt .45 revolver about her person. The leather gauntlets later came into Brian's possession and he made good use of them when he became a square dance caller and decided to dress the part, as will be seen in a later chapter.

As in all families, anecdotes passed down from parent to child run alongside the official documents. Brian remembers hearing that his grandfather was a travelling boot and shoe salesman. And indeed, in the 1891 census Edgar was listed as a 'warehouseman' lodging in Barnes, south west London which is consistent with what Brian had been told. The word 'warehouseman' had various connotations. It could mean someone who worked in a shop (literally a 'ware-house') or a wholesale merchant, particularly one dealing with textiles.

There are scant clues as to the development of Edgar Sherriff's career within the scrapbook – but one letter has survived, guaranteed to raise a smile, tucked between its pages. When Edgar was away on business, he and his wife corresponded by letter. One letter has been preserved and the contents suggest that the couple wrote to each other on an almost daily basis. The letter is written in black ink on cream paper. No date is given, just a weekday and a time. It seems to have been written in two instalments on consecutive days. In the letter Edgar addresses his wife by her nickname 'Bert'.

Central Hotel
Dublin
Wednesday night 10.30

My dearest Bert,
Just arrived here and received your two letters, glad to hear you are getting along alright, and that the children are such pretty beauties. I have had nothing but misfortune. My top hat that I did up so carefully in a parcel I left in the train at Leeds. Is it worth writing for? I had to buy a felt hat in Cork. I left my gloves at Killarney and had to write and tell them to forward on to Belfast, and then tonight I left my umbrella behind at Limerick and have written to send on to Belfast. I shall lose my coat off my back next I suppose. It has kept beautifully fine today and the sun has been very hot. I am now off to bed. So good night.

Dublin
Thursday 1.45

Still more losses, coming up from Limerick. I left my pipe in the carriage, so shall have to buy a new one. I have finished here and shall get on by 2.25 for Belfast where I will write you when to expect me. Have done very well here as usual. I had your letter of yesterday this morning. Must close now.

Yours ever, Edgar

P.S. Tell the children I will try to write them tomorrow.

It's astonishing that this successful man was in the habit of travelling with such absentminded abandon. What comes across, however, is his easy intimacy with his wife and his cheerful confidence: 'Have done very well here as usual.'

An interesting companion-piece to this is a letter written by Kay when young. It was also found pressed between two pages of the book of cuttings. It's a typical child's letter. Lines have been ruled indifferently with a blunt pencil to help Kay with her joined-up writing. She has started off in red ink, then changed to black, then pencil. Obviously the abundance of the letter 'y' in the names of her two younger sisters led her to get carried away with the looping letters of her cursive script.

> *My dear Mother,*
> *I hope you are enjoying yourself. We have just finished dinner and we are just going to post this letter. You can come home whenever you like. Gladys sendys her love and twelve kisses and Phyllis sendys her love and twelve kisses. Dear Mother.*
>
> *Kathleen*

Whilst this is a charming document in its own right, it also sheds light on part of the family history. By chance, Kay has used her father's headed paper for the letter providing a vital clue for dating his association with the corset factory. At the top of the page is printed: 'George Langridge and Co (EJ Sherriff), St George's Stay Factory, Church Road, St George, Bristol'. The full date has not been included, but is printed as 189–, with the last digit left blank to be filled in by hand. It is a tantalising omission.

It is thought that Edgar Sherriff acquired the corset factory in 1894 and this letter could have provided corroboration. In any case in 1901 Edgar's occupation was recorded in the national census not as 'warehouseman' but as 'corset manufacturer'. The family story had begun and its origins lay in Bristol.

5

Raising the Dust

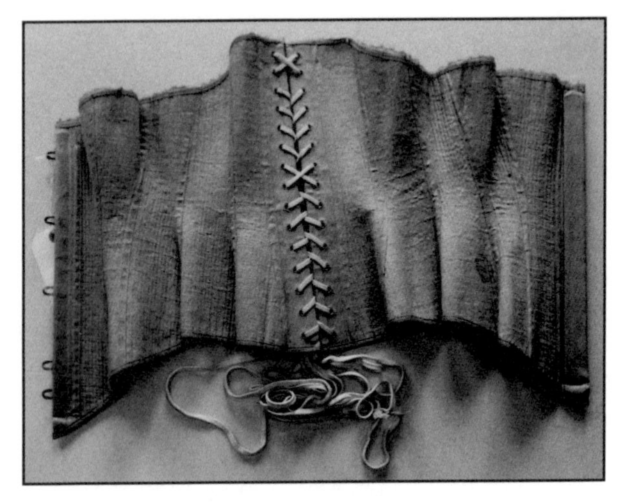

A corset from the Langridge Ltd collection

Raising The Dust

All cities have a layered history, but it is rare for this to be quite so apparent as it is in Bristol. A good example of this is Castle Park, which takes its name from a real castle. Its first incarnation was a motte-and-bailey castle built in the eleventh century. This was subsequently rebuilt and modified over the years and finally destroyed as a result of an Act of Parliament in the mid-seventeenth century.

On the site of the castle a flourishing commercial centre grew up. Centuries later, this was razed to the ground in the Bristol blitz of November 1940. Now it is a park, the largest green space within the city centre, and – by a strange circularity of fate – the ruins of the castle have been revealed once again.

I visit Bristol to retrace the origins of the factory bought by Edgar Sherriff and my search begins at Castle Street. Castle Street and Queen Street cut into the south-east border of the park and it is here the factory once stood more than two hundred years ago.

According to Sherriff family legend, Langridge Ltd was founded by a woman and was not at first involved in the business of making corsets, but stockings. There appear to be no records going back this far and Brian's word-of-mouth testimony may be the only trace left of these early origins. The earliest listing for the business in Bristol trade directories is in 1816 where it is given as 'Langridge, Richard, Stay and Corset Maker, Wholesale and Retail.' The address is 63 Castle Street.

In fact, the factory moved many times in its early years, but most of the addresses are clustered around this area, bordering what is now the park. I decide to walk, as if along a timeline, from Castle Street to Bridge Street to Wine Street. And from there to Temple Street, the factory's location in the 1870s and 1880s.

It is almost dusk and, as I cut across the green space, I stop to take in the ruins of the castle. Bicycles glide by, silently but very fast, dazzling me with their front lights. A bat flits over my head. As I make the rounds of the park, I can see no trace of the buildings that might once have housed the corset factory. This is probably explained by the fact that the entire district was heavily bombed during the Second World War.

From Wine Street, I make my way to Temple Street, and there I am presented with a problem. Temple Street lies on the street map of Bristol like two fragments of snipped ribbon, the central section now lost beneath Victoria Street. A false lead has me asking questions in two pubs which lie on what remains of Temple Street, *The King's Head* and *The Cornubia*. Although the beer is flowing, my questions are not unwelcome. In *The King's Head,* the bartender seems delighted, and not even very surprised, to be asked about a corset factory in the late 1800s. In *The Cornubia* I am told that the premises have been standing since 1775 (as is proudly painted on the building's exterior) and that there were originally two houses on the site, where wigs were made by fishermen's wives.

The mention of fishermen's wives is pertinent, as these women are known to have been the mainstay of the textile industry along the British coastline, the leap from fishing to corsetry not being as great as may at first be supposed. I make note of the few remaining house numbers for Temple Street and conclude that the site of the old factory is probably beneath tarmac.

Just as Temple Street seems to have nothing more to offer, I am stopped short by the discovery of a grand stone archway with a vista through to Temple Church. Across the top of the archway is written 'The Temple or Holy Cross'. The Portland stone of the archway has been eaten away, but the destruction has been of the slow, inevitable kind, unlike the destruction of the church. Through the archway I can see Temple Church and it takes my breath away. The tower is still standing, but at an angle. Where stained glass would once have filled the windows, there is now only sky, the royal blue rapidly darkening into black. The floor of the church is all grass. It seems incongruous in a city of such prosperity, such a modern, vibrant city, to see this hollow shell, a reminder of war-time sorrow.

The church is lit by an orange streetlamp and as I approach it I can smell decay. A mounted notice tells me what I need to know. Temple Church was bombed on 24 November 1940. A medieval map of Bristol takes me even further back:

Temple Street, the way it once was, a single unbroken road. With a jolt of recognition I see racks used by weavers to hang out their cloth marked on the hand-drawn map. Even in medieval times, this part of Bristol had been a place for working with cloth. I later find out the reason for the name Temple Church; the original church on the site was built by the Knights Templar. A naive sixteenth century map of 'Brightstowe' shows how Temple Street once led directly to Temple Gate, an actual gate in the city wall.

I visit the next known site of the corset factory the following day, 248a Church Road, St George. Here, I know, the factory flourished within living memory. This was where Brian's grandfather, then his father, both worked as owners and directors of Langridge Ltd corset factory. It is the site of the factory Brian visited as a child and the place he later worked as a young man. The location is easy to find. The factory site is bordered by two roads with evocative names, Seneca Street and Ebenezer Street. I walk down Seneca Street, round the corner into Ebenezer Street and see that the building in question is covered in scaffolding and brick-red mesh. There is the hollow sound of hammering from inside and dust is being raised.

As I peer through the scaffolding, I can see that the building is being refitted for new ownership. The builders are happy to talk and fill me in on the recent history of the place. After it ceased to be a corset factory it was for a period an oriental food factory and, most recently, 'film studios', they tell me somewhat sheepishly. They add that, as they've been sifting through the rubble, they've come across glamour DVDs and revealing shots of women. It's not exactly what I was hoping to find.

I ask if they have unearthed any remnants of its days as a corset factory or even further back, when the building was a dance hall and theatre. But the workmen have found nothing from those earlier days, no theatre props, no Singer sewing machine parts, not so much as a bobbin.

Before Brian's grandfather bought the corset factory it belonged to its founders, the Langridge family. The enterprise was so successful that it's unlikely Edgar Sherriff would ever have had the opportunity to buy the business, had it not been for an unexpected tragedy. In 1851 George Langridge died of a heart attack. He was just 56 years of age.

The death was recorded in the local papers in the following terms: 'Awfully sudden death. It is our melancholy duty this week to record the death, under painfully sudden circumstances, of one of our principal manufacturing tradesmen, Mr George Langridge. Mr Langridge had recently emerged from a severe and dangerous illness and it was hoped that he was progressing favourably towards recovery. On Sunday he was able to drive out in his pony phaeton...'

This improvement, however, was only to be temporary. The account finishes with a distinctly Victorian tableau as Langridge spoke his last words. 'Addressing a son and daughter, who were in attendance upon him, he faintly articulated, "Love one another" and almost immediately expired.'

He left nine children behind him.

In the year of his death, the business was possibly at the height of its success, employing 230 people in the factory and related outlets. George's eldest son James inherited the business and quickly enlisted the help of his brother Richard. An auction was held, perhaps to raise capital. The brothers ran the business successfully for more than two decades, but by 1875 they were failing to make a profit and the two men faced ruin.

The factory continued in different manifestations for a few more years before in 1886 the buildings at Temple Street were put up for auction, with the successors of George Langridge and Co retaining 'a moiety of the premises' in which to run the corsetry business.

It was at this point that Edgar Sherriff, bicyclist, boot and shoe salesman, absent-minded traveller and affectionate husband, entered the picture. This must have been when the event took place which subsequently entered into Sherriff family mythology: the day the machinists in their long sweeping skirts, most of them not much older than fifteen, picked up their Singer sewing machines, boarded the tram and made their way to the new location of the factory: 248a Church Road, St George, Bristol. When Brian says the address, it sounds like an incantation.

6

Two Soldiers

Bernard's regiment

Two Soldiers

Of Edgar Sherriff's six children, Bernard, the oldest son, was the natural heir to the corsetry business. It was his misfortune to celebrate his twenty-first birthday on 1 August 1914, just a few days after war was declared. He enlisted at once.

Like his father, he was an active man, but it was a horse he rode into battle, not a bicycle. He was a sergeant in the Royal Field Artillery. A photograph still exists of soldiers from his regiment. Thirty or so men and their well-groomed horses stand in the foreground, arrayed over a field of scrubby grass. Behind them, gun carriages can be seen towed on limbers. To the left-hand side of the image is a solitary man on horseback. To the right, a caravan of horses and men drifts on into the distance. Bernard Sherriff is thought to be in the photograph, which has been kept faithfully by his family, but he remains unidentified. The names of the soldiers have not been recorded and there is no indication of the date or the location of the scene, although Larkhill near Salisbury has been suggested. The sepia image has the lazy contentment of an English summer afternoon. Nobody is standing to attention and the men and horses are not in line. The grass has been allowed to grow long. This, when viewed with the hindsight of a century, was a time of relative innocence. Devastation on the scale that would shortly follow was unimaginable.

On Sunday 9 December 1928 a play with the title *Journey's End* was staged for the first time at the Apollo Theatre in the West End of London, with a young Laurence Olivier in the role of Captain Stanhope. There was just one evening performance scheduled and one matinee, an indication of the modest expectations of all involved.

The play was a risky proposition. It was one of the first plays to be staged after the end of the First World War showing the life of officers in the trenches as it really was, stripped of patriotic glamour. The focus of the drama is on the minutiae of daily life in a dugout and the fierce friendships that developed in that terrible situation, poised between life and death. It is about stoicism as much as heroism and the play unfolds as an understated, unbearable tragedy. The playwright was Robert Cedric Sherriff, or RC Sherriff as he is widely known. He was Bernard's cousin. There are certain parallels in the two men's experiences of war although the outcomes were very different.

RC Sherriff was working as an insurance clerk when he decided to enlist. He joined the Artists Rifles in November 1915, a regiment which had been founded in 1860 in response to a perceived threat of French invasion. Early members were the painters Edward Burne-Jones, William Holman Hunt and Dante Gabriel Rossetti. The regiment later attracted poets such as Edward Thomas and Wilfred Owen and artists including the brothers Paul and John Nash. RC Sherriff served with the 9th Battalion of the East Surrey Regiment from October 1916. He was wounded at Passchendaele near Ypres in August 1917 and was invalided out.

After the war, RC Sherriff returned to work as an insurance clerk and began to write plays in his spare time, as a way of raising funds for Kingston Rowing Club, of which he was a loyal supporter.

However, *Journey's End* defied all expectations and its phenomenal success in both Europe and America meant that he was able to leave his job at the insurance company and become a full-time writer. His best-selling novel, *The Fortnight in September*, earned him an invitation to Hollywood. He went on to write and co-write numerous screenplays. His hugely creative output in subsequent years included *The Invisible Man, Goodbye Mr Chips*, adapted from the novel of the same name by James Hilton, and *The Dam Busters*.

Bernard's life unfolded differently. With the Royal Field Artillery he was posted to France and Belgium and saw for himself the consequences of a war that straddled the old world and the new. The time for heroic charges was over. The horses were ill-suited to modern military tactics and men and horses alike became easy targets.

Like his cousin, Bernard was sent back to England with war wounds in 1917. He was reunited with his wife Dorothy for a short period only. Whether he was able to return home or whether she visited him in hospital has not been recorded. However, he probably would have lived long enough to learn that he was going to be a father.

Bernard died in Southern General Hospital in Bristol from 'wounds received'. It was known by the family that he had pneumonia. His only child, a daughter Bernice, was born the following year.

Bernard's untimely death changed everything for his brother Jack. He was now the only boy in the family, which meant that the corset factory would one day be his. Jack, who was thirteen years old when war broke out and seventeen when it came to an end, had narrowly missed his chance of active combat, but conscription continued into peacetime and Jack went on to join his late brother's regiment.

On the day Jack married Joan, the Royal Artillery presented him with a silver cigarette case with a flurry of signatures engraved onto the lid. Bernard would not have been far from his thoughts. Bernard's daughter Bernice was a bridesmaid at the wedding and can be seen in their wedding portrait.

7

On the Other Side of the Curtain

Brian's mother Joan

On the Other Side of the Curtain

Although Jack was a good father, he could be stern. Brian remembers feeling very small and his father's voice being very loud. His mother provided a counterweight to this sternness. He remembers her as 'just what a mother should be – kind'.

With his mother, a German nursemaid Ingfried and his brother Tony to play with, Brian's early childhood was a happy one. His favourite toys were a jointed crocodile made of tin, which could be wound up with a key and made a ticking sound as it moved along, and a metal snake of a similar design. Then, as he grew older, there were the model railways.

Brian's father loved model railways as much as the boys did. The first, a Hornby 'O' gauge railway set with a wind-up engine and trucks, was so large that it took up the entire living room floor. Joan complained that this made it rather difficult for her to do the cleaning. The wind-up railway set was superseded by an electric one, a Hornby 'OO' gauge, complete with a Caerphilly Castle engine, coaches and trucks. This one was placed on a table and screwed down. Brian remembers these times playing with trains as providing rare moments of understanding between father and son.

Brian's childhood was unusual by any account. For one thing, his parents were in the habit of attending meetings with spiritualists. Brian would sometimes accompany them. One medium, aptly named Mr Strange, was a manual labourer with a strong Bath accent. When Brian and his parents arrived for a séance, they would find the room decked out in black cloth. Brian remembers a round table and a cup turned upside down. If someone asked a question, the cup would travel.

As a young boy, Brian had not been impressed by these close encounters with the departed. In fact he used to get a bit bored. However, the influence of spiritualism was to stay with him all his life. When he later came to build a home for himself, he would name it after his spirit guide.

Spiritualism had a surge of popularity in the early 1920s and 1930s, perhaps a natural response to the loss of life brought about by the First World War. The endorsement of some prominent figures, including Arthur Conan Doyle, also lent respectability to spiritualism. At the time of Joan and Jack's marriage there were probably a quarter of a million practising spiritualists in Britain.

As well as consulting mediums, Brian's mother wrote spiritual poetry. Her extended poem, *The Temple of The Sacred Heart*, was printed by Camborne Printing and Stationery Company. It is both dreamlike and mystical.

Years later, Brian and his parents visited a medium called Dolly who lived in St Merryn, Cornwall. Dolly would conduct séances in the company of a younger woman named Vi, who handled the business end of the proceedings. The house opposite Dolly's had a reputation for hauntings and Brian always hoped and feared to hear the ghost of a horseman who was said to ride across the roof.

As Brian describes the scene to me, a door in the room where we are sitting closes unexpectedly.

'The spiritualists would say, "Thank you, Friend",' Brian tells me.

A more conventional pastime was provided by visits to Jack's mother, Bertha, who had once been the recipient of Edgar's affectionate letters and went on to outlive her husband by twenty-two years. In Brian's eyes his grandmother seemed very strict, 'a Victorian really'. On visits to her house, Brian, his brother and their cousin Jeffrey would be confined to one half of a room, which was divided by a dark blue curtain. The grown-ups would talk about matters that were not deemed suitable for young ears and play cards. For the children there were Dinky Toy cars, a rocking horse and a doll's house. The latter they barely touched, considering it something for girls, but they did drive the toy cars all over the floors and walls. As they played, the three boys could hear the crackle and deep hum of records placed on the gramophone on the other side of the curtain, cheerful dance music and more soulful classical arrangements.

For Brian, the gramophone was a great source of fascination. It was housed within a cabinet on four legs. Brian was not allowed to play with it, but it was enough for him just to open and shut the cabinet doors, which had the effect of increasing and decreasing the volume. When the gramophone was turned off, he liked to put his head inside the cabinet. The sound-board was lined with velvet.

Visits to Brian's maternal grandparents were more frequent. To enter their house, it was necessary to go down some steps to a door in the basement. As far as Brian could tell, Grandma and Grandpa Millman dwelt permanently in the basement of their home, even though they had a perfectly adequate upper floor. In fact, a whole storey of their house, boasting the finest furniture, china and ornaments was kept only 'for best'.

Brian's grandmother usually greeted him wearing a flowery apron. Just behind her on the table would be a freshly baked cottage loaf for tea-time. This consisted of two tiers of white bread. The smaller loaf on top was always for Brian. While this cosy domestic scene was taking place, Grandpa Millman, a man of shortish build with brown hair and a moustache, would usually slip out to the pub.

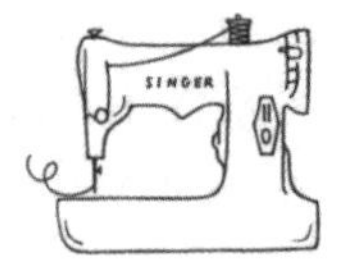
SINGER

8

Music While You Work

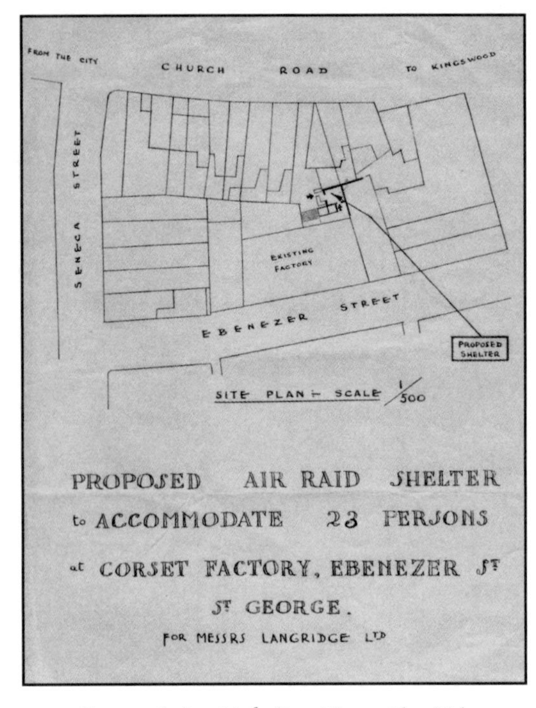

Proposed air raid shelter at Langridge Ltd

Music While You Work

Brian's family was living at 1 Hanbury Road, Clifton, a leafy residential district of Bristol, when war broke out. Brian was eleven years old. He was a pupil at Marlborough House School. He used to walk to school every day and the war didn't change that. Every morning Brian set off with his satchel and a small brown carboard box containing a gas mask slung over his shoulder.

Once again Jack was not called up to fight for his country. This was despite the fact that he had been a voluntary member of the Territorial Army for years, having never forgotten his brother's sacrifice. As a factory owner, Jack was in what was called a 'reserved occupation'. Even in wartime women needed underwear!

Instead, Jack joined the Local Defence Volunteers, which later came to be known as the Home Guard. There was no uniform to begin with, just an arm band which read 'LDV'.

He was one of a motley band of men

preparing for the unthinkable in complete earnest. Brian used to help his father attend to the horses.

At the factory, instead of singing, the machinists now listened to *Music While You Work* on the radio, which was broadcast by the BBC for half an hour in the morning and half an hour in the afternoon. This featured cheerful music by bands such as Troise and His Banjoliers.

Plans were drawn up for an air-raid shelter for the factory, but before these could be implemented, the building was requisitioned. It was assigned to Pitman Books as a warehouse. The corset factory was on the move again.

Jack and his staff were relocated a couple of miles east, to the site of an offshoot of Langridge Ltd on Two Mile Hill. This was Langridge (Kingswood) Ltd, which had been established in 1920, as the result of a collaboration between Edgar Sherriff and a man named Sidney Ryall. By the time of the relocation, Sidney's son Charles was running the business – with considerable flair. Charles later renamed the business Unity Corset Factories and set up a marketing company, Fantasie Foundations.

When Jack and Charles were discussing business matters, Brian would usually be asked to leave the room. This was something he resented. However, he did once manage to overhear something of interest. Whilst eavesdropping, he was amazed to hear the two directors talking about an old stable in Keynsham which contained an unallocated supply of fabric – and this at a time of strict rationing!

Langridge Ltd supported the war effort by manufacturing parachutes and supplying the Women's Auxiliary Air Force (WAAFs) and Women's Royal Naval Service (WRNS) with panty-girdles. In 1943 the Kingswood site was honoured with a visit from Queen Mary.

Jack told his family that as the Queen was shown around the factory and various items were laid out before her she only had to say the words 'I like this' to be given a sample to take away with her. She left with rather a good haul.

Brian returned to 248a Church Road, St George just once during the war years. He wanted to see what had happened to the factory after it was requisitioned. He peeked through a window. The deserted interior shimmered with dust and he could see stacks of books covering the whole area and rising from floor to ceiling.

To begin with, the raids were a novelty. When the first bombs fell, the whole family piled into Jack's beige Chrysler and made an outing of it. They wanted to see for themselves. When they reached the first damaged building, split open like a doll's house, there was already a steady stream of cars passing by. The boys stood up in the back seat and looked out of the sunshine roof. Hundreds of miles away in Germany, German mothers and fathers and children were doing much the same thing.

Bristol, due to its importance as a port and manufacturing centre, was marked out as a target for German bombers. The river Avon made Bristol particularly vulnerable to attack, guiding airmen to the city as surely as an arrow on a moonlit night.

For Brian, the first effects of wartime he noticed were at school. The finest young teachers left to serve in the Army, Navy and Air Force. Class sizes increased and those members of staff who were left behind weren't always the most charismatic.

The power balance between pupils and teachers shifted in the pupils' favour and a short season of mayhem ensued. In one particular incident, ink-soaked blotting-paper pellets were thrown. Brian was singled out and made to sit in the corridor wearing a dunce's cap with the letter D marked upon it. He does not feel any particular shame, reliving this. At the time he simply accepted that it was his turn to be punished.

In September 1940 Brian moved up to Clifton College Preparatory School, although his time there was to be short-lived. As autumn progressed, the raids on Bristol ceased to be the stuff of family outings.

Academic lessons were punctuated with lessons in survival, none of which Brian took very seriously. During gas mask drills, he was delighted to discover that if he blew out while wearing a mask, he could make a rude noise. An intermittent wailing sound meant a trip to the air-raid shelter in the school grounds, a dome-shaped bunker lined with sandbags. Inside, rows of benches had been laid out. Teachers and pupils hunkered down together and waited for the 'all clear' to sound its long single note.

One afternoon, Brian had an experience that was to stay with him for the rest of his life. He was sitting in class staring out of the window, when an airman floated out of the sky on a parachute. Brian was fascinated. He wondered what it must have been like for the airman to see the city from above. Brian presumed the man had bailed out of a dogfight in the sky. He never discovered if it was an Englishman or a German who had floated down that day and, for reasons he does not quite understand, Brian never said anything to anyone about what he had seen.

Brian's school was close to Bristol Zoo and he often heard the lions roaring when he was in class. His walk to and from school brought him close to the zoo and he loved to make a detour to see the animals and the zookeepers in their caps. His favourite inhabitant was a gorilla named Alfred. In Brian's opinion, Alfred's cage was too small for him, although there was a door at the back, which led to a sleeping area. During the day, Alfred used to grip one bar in his left hand and one bar in his right and stare out at the world with a philosophical expression.

Zoo animals were particularly vulnerable during raids. When the bombs fell in Europe, there were tales of leopards and lions roaming the capital cities and of exotic animals being caught and used in the cooking pot, because food was scarce. Many zoos including London Zoo took the precaution of evacuating their most valuable animals to less prominent locations. In cities around the world animals in captivity were put down, sometimes shot, to avoid a more painful death by fire or starvation. At Bristol Zoo the leopards and tigers were evacuated, along with one elephant, but a pair of lions remained and it was probably these animals that Brian heard.

On the night of 24 November 1940, Brian was at home with his parents, just about to go to bed, when the air raid siren sounded. Joan, Jack, Brian and Tony made their way to the air raid shelter in the cellar of their house, expecting a relatively quiet night.

Inside the shelter, a bunk-bed had been fitted for the boys. The bedstead reached right up to the ceiling, providing extra reinforcement against bomb damage – at least that was the theory. Brian climbed up to the top bunk and Tony got into the lower one. Brian felt cosy under the tightly-stretched sheet and blanket, knowing that he was surrounded by his family. As he drifted off to sleep, he listened to the sound of aeroplanes. He was able to identify enemy aircraft; the sound they made was uneven, questing, as if they were trying to decide where to drop their bombs. They were close.

And pretty soon Brian could hear the bombs start to fall, each one screaming down with a high-pitched whine, followed a moment later by a deep, rumbling crash. The 'all clear' sounded just after midnight, but by then Brian was asleep. He barely registered as he was lifted by his father, carried upstairs and put into his own bed.

The following day Brian walked to school as usual. In his immediate neighbourhood he saw nothing out of the ordinary – at first. And yet everything was different. He could smell smoke and fire and the lions in the zoo were roaring.

It would not have been an exaggeration to say the city was on fire. Fire brigades from all over the country were brought in to quench the flames. This was the night on which Bristol's commercial centre went up in flames and Temple Church was burnt from the inside out. There were more than two hundred deaths and almost seven hundred people were injured. Men and women took to the streets with shovels to clear the fallen masonry and dig out survivors, corpses and body parts from the rubble.

The enemy's plan was to eliminate Bristol's capabilities as a port in order to reduce imports to the country as a whole. Although the British media underplayed their coverage of the events of 24 November, it had been catastrophic for Bristol.

Brian and Tony were kept away from the worst affected areas. Instead, they were busy gleaning their locality for shrapnel and keeping a look-out for the biggest prize, an incendiary bomb case. One of these could be traded for any number of pieces of shrapnel at school.

Eight days later, just as a measure of normality had been resumed, there was another major raid. Once again Brian spent the night in the air raid shelter. The noises were louder this time. He listened hard to see if he could identify British or enemy aircraft. It was impossible to sleep but he wasn't frightened.

The following morning, as he walked to school, light-headed from lack of sleep, he saw an Italian prisoner of war wandering the streets, similarly in a daze. He was identifiable by the brown blouse he wore, with a yellow circle sewn onto the back. Brian turned the corner onto Pembroke Road and there he saw a church on fire. He was so surprised by the sight that he walked into a lamp-post and bumped his nose.

The church was one he'd been familiar with all his life, although he'd never stepped inside. It was All Saints, a high church. He'd always been fascinated by the bells he heard ringing within its walls and the lingering smell of incense. Today black smoke was billowing out.

Some of the buildings at Clifton College were damaged in the raid that night and the decision was made to evacuate the pupils at Brian's school to Bude on Cornwall's north coast. Places for evacuees were limited and as Brian was new to the school, he was not selected to travel with the other pupils to Bude. Instead, in January 1941, his whole family moved to Saltford, Somerset.

Unknown to Brian, Saltford was also the home of a girl named Patricia Harvey, who would one day become his wife.

9

Condor and Kestrel

Boats at Saltford on the River Avon – a photograph from Brian's childhood

Condor and Kestrel

Brian and his family hadn't moved far – Jack was still able to travel to the factory every day – but it was far enough. Saltford is situated between Bristol and Bath. From the front garden of their new home, it was possible to see the red glare in the sky over Bristol, and from their back garden, the red glare in the sky over Bath as bombs fell. By contrast, Saltford was a haven of tranquillity.

Their new home was a bungalow called *Water Row*, aptly named as it was on the banks of the River Avon. On the day of their arrival, Brian was the first to dash inside the house. He discovered that there was no electricity. Instead of electric lights, there were gas lamps; these had delicate white mantels which increased in size when the lamps were turned on. He was completely entranced by them.

The next morning the milkman pulled up outside the bungalow in a small horse-drawn cart. Joan searched through half-unloaded crates to find a jug, which she carried outside to him. The milkman used a dipper to ladle milk from his churn. After breakfast, which included large glasses of milk for everyone, Brian and Tony went out to explore.

Over the next few days, they made it their business to get to know their surroundings. They discovered that at the end of Mead Lane there was a pub, *The Jolly Sailor,* and a village shop so crammed with out-of-date magazines that it was hard for the shopkeeper to make her way to the counter to sell sweets. They walked along the river and explored the lock. They saw three barges: the gaily-painted Avon King and Avon Queen and a rather dirty tar barge, The Jolly. At Saltford railway station, they put pennies on the line, and then retreated just in time to see the Bristol to London steam train roaring through, flattening the coins. Their pennies flew off and landed at the side of the track, paper-thin, but double the diameter.

Brian had barely got used to his new home when he realised he would soon be moving out. He walked into the room he shared with his brother one day and found his mother packing a trunk for him. He was to be a boarder at Monkton Combe School and term was about to begin. She carefully folded his school uniform and asked him what he'd like to put in the trunk. He decided upon some pieces of shrapnel to impress the other boys and a notebook for newspaper cuttings. Two days later, when Brian opened the trunk in his new school dormitory, he found that his mother had sneaked a tin of biscuits inside.

At first, Brian was unsettled in his new school. It was his first time living away from home and he knew it would be a month before he could request permission for a weekend's leave. He sleepwalked. The dormitory he slept in was above the gymnasium and somehow Brian managed to navigate along a corridor, down the stairs and into the gymnasium, all while fast asleep. The first thing he knew of it was when he bumped into a leather punch-bag suspended from the ceiling and woke up.

Brian was not very studious and had no particular ambitions. He was keen on French and Geography, having visited France a couple of times with his parents before the war, and he liked Latin, but that was it.

He also found chapel very dull. Every weekend there was homework to do, sport (at which he did not excel) and chapel. Whenever he could, he spent the duration of chapel up in the organ loft turning pages for one of the boys. At other times, he risked punishment and went to the shed where the animals were kept, hoping his absence wouldn't be noticed. Each boy was allowed to keep one pet, most of which the boys had caught in the wild. Brian's pet was a grass snake.

Brian's happiest times were spent out of doors. He became friends with a boy named Paul Holman and on Sunday afternoons the boys requested permission to leave the school grounds. They cycled out to explore the surrounding area. Paul had a pet jackdaw and the jackdaw came with them. It sat on the handlebars of Paul's bicycle as they cycled along. Sometimes it took off and Paul would call it back again. It always returned, which impressed Brian greatly. Better than a grass snake.

Sometimes the two boys visited Keen's Tea Shop where Mrs Keen, a plump white-haired lady, served them cream teas.

Another favourite destination was Midford, where the old railway station had assumed an important role in the public imagination. *The Ghost Train,* directed by Walter Forde and screened in 1941, had been filmed there. The film, based on a play by Arnold Ridley, is a war-time ghost story, in which the last steam train from London to Cornwall becomes stranded at a deserted railway station.

When the time came for Brian's first weekend's leave, Jack collected him in the car. However, at dinner that night Brian's parents explained that as he was eleven, soon to be twelve, he could make the journey alone next time.

When his next weekend's leave came around, Brian got up before dawn, determined to make the best use of his free time. It was still dark when he set off. His route took him along narrow leafy lanes, which had no lighting of any kind. There was rustling and whispering in the trees and in the absolute blackness Brian could see ghostly faces between the leaves. He pushed his fists into his pockets and kept on walking, even though he could hear his own heart pounding. Looking neither left nor right and barely daring to breathe, he made his way up over the top of the hill and down the other side. By the time he reached *Water Row*, the sun had risen and the landscape looked bright, beautiful and perfectly harmless. He never mentioned the incident to his parents.

On his twelfth birthday, Brian received a gift, the best gift he could possibly have asked for: his own canoe. It was a Folbot, a very popular folding canoe which could easily be carried when not on the water. Brian named it Condor. Tony received his own canoe three months later on his tenth birthday. He named his Kestrel. Now weekends were transformed. Brian and Tony were able to launch their canoes on the River Avon, which could be reached by crossing the road in front of their bungalow. The whole of Somerset belonged to them.

In the years that followed, they would paddle up and down the River Avon, over the Dundas Aqueduct and on the Kennet and Avon canals. Brian sometimes paddled as far as Pulteney Bridge in Bath – a breathtakingly beautiful construction with shops along its length, often compared to the Ponte Vecchio in Florence.

Once Brian paddled all the way from home to school. The journey took him almost five hours and he wrote an account of it for the school magazine. Intensely black full stops and exclamation marks show that it was hammered out by hand on a typewriter. A friend named Simon joined him on the first part of the journey.

'I considered myself exceptionally lucky to obtain leave from the headmaster to bring Condor back to Monkton Combe by the Avon,' the account begins. 'At 3.15pm Simon and I left Saltford in Condor and Kingfisher bound for the School Boathouse 15 miles upstream. We had a good following wind as far as Saltford Weir, which we reached without undue effort. This weir can easily be negotiated, either by portaging over the lock or sliding the canoe over the end of the weir, where the drop is gradual. Above the weir, there is a long straight stretch, one mile in length, excellent for sailing if there is a wind. Although we had no sails, the wind made us fly along.'

Brian remembered that it was on this stretch of the river that tragedy had struck the previous year. The helmsman of the Avon King, whom Brian knew quite well by this time, had passed too close to the branches of an overhanging tree and been pulled into the water and drowned.

It was as Brian considered these gloomy matters that Simon announced he had to go home for his tea, so Brian continued the journey alone. The landscape changed, imperceptibly at first, until he found himself in the heart of industrial Bath. There was oil and a fine coating of soot floating on the water. He continued as slowly as he could, trying to avoid the debris and filth. As he passed under Old Bridge, a stone whizzed past his ear and plopped into the water just a foot in front of him. He became aware of laughter. He had an audience. The current suddenly picked up and, as he struggled to keep control of the canoe, he heard jeering.

'Nothing hit me,' he later typed philosophically, 'and I reached Pulteney Weir with the canoe still in one piece.' The account concluded with a romantic touch, a wistful reference to Warleigh Weir. 'It was dusk when I passed and I missed its beauty.'

Finally Brian made it to school, '27 minutes late, after a journey of four hours 42 minutes'.

Like his grandfather, Brian was in the habit of pasting newspaper cuttings into scrapbooks, usually old school exercise books. He was a cox in the first eight at Monkton Combe and the 'Bumps' Races featured prominently. He was in a house called 'Farm' and he underlined any small triumphs experienced by Farm in blue ink.

In one such book, dated March 1942, photographs of boats are interspersed with images of war: military tanks, aeroplanes (a Junkers 88 and a Vultee dive-bomber), a Russian air-sledge and several pages of motorbikes. There are cartoons, *Believe It or Not …* by Ripley, and at the back a rather sultry photograph of Dorothy Lamour. In one cutting, there's an image of a soldier in a tin helmet rearing up on the back wheel of his bike; he appears to be going over the top of the trenches.

Brian was under no illusions. He fully expected to be going to war as soon as he left school.

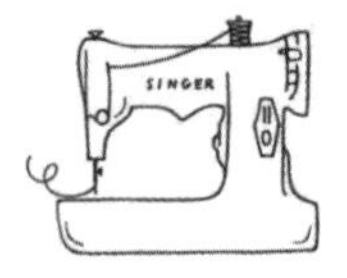
SINGER

10

Surrender

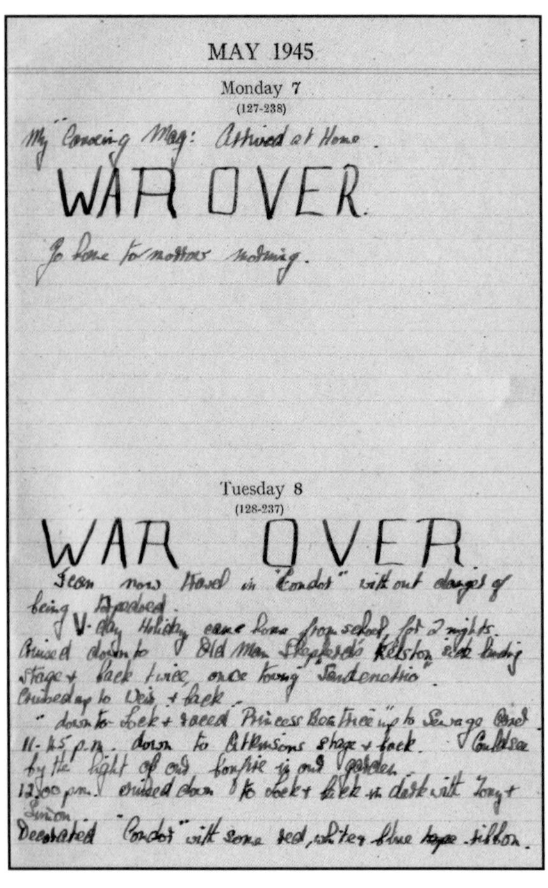

MAY 1945

Monday 7
(127-238)

My "Canoeing Mag: Arrived at Home.

WAR OVER.

Go home to-morrow morning.

Tuesday 8
(128-237)

WAR OVER

I can now travel in "Condor" without danger of being torpedoed.
V-day Holiday came home from school for 2 nights.
Cruised down to Old Man Shepherd's Kelston side landing stage + back twice, once towing "[illegible]".
Cruised up to Weir + back.
" down to lock + raced "Princess Beatrice" up to Sewage Bend.
11-45 p.m. down to Atkinsons stage + back. Could see by the light of our bonfire in our garden.
12.00 p.m. cruised down to lock + back in dark with Tony + Simon.
Decorated "Condor" with some red, white + blue tape ribbon.

The log book Brian kept for Condor

Surrender

It was the end of an ordinary afternoon at home with his family. Brian sneaked past the garage, hoping to wipe some of the mud off his clothes before his mother caught sight of him. But something stopped him in his tracks. His father was lying on the concrete floor of the garage. His mother was kneeling by his side.

Brian watched his mother pulling at his father's lifeless shoulders. She looked up.

'He's only gone and gassed himself,' she said.

Bit by bit, she managed to manoeuvre his body out of the doorway into the fresh air. The flow of time slowed and stopped. Brian was still standing motionless when his father's eyes fluttered and opened. Unobserved, Tony had sidled up to join them and was watching, wide-eyed.

Afterwards, Joan explained to Brian how she'd been in the kitchen and had suddenly felt that she should check on her husband. Jack had been in the garage working on his car with the engine running and no doors open.

'A thing you must never do,' Joan said. He had almost died from carbon monoxide poisoning. She had found him just in time.

At school Brian was busy learning the craft of war. He was a member of the Junior Training Corps and, later, the Officers Training Corps. For this he was given a First World War uniform with serge wool trousers that ended just below the knee and puttees that had to be wound round his shins. He had to polish his brass buttons with a button stick, a little shield which slipped under the buttons to protect the uniform from polish.

He underwent a basic military training and received a certificate endorsed by the War Office. This confirmed that he, 'the cadet', had reached the required fitness levels and had shown proficiency in drill and weapon training with a rifle and a Sten gun (a lightweight machine gun). After training each day, Brian remembers that one teacher used to shower in the nude in full view of the boys, attracting their curious stares.

Brian's passion for his canoe had not waned as he grew older – quite the opposite. When he was sixteen, he bought a log book which he kept with military precision. At the front he wrote in purple ink: 'Log Book of Canoe Condor. Master: BJ Sherriff.' At the back, he kept a record of all his navigational expenses. These included a subscription for the Canoeing Club, a Folbot handbook, a rope, two pots of silver paint for the tips of his paddles, one pot of light green Cuprinol for the deck, a small Merlin tent, an air cushion, lock fees and camp site fees. With others in the Canoeing Club, he would paddle out and camp along the side of the river Avon. Brian kept his log book assiduously and lavished affection on Condor that might normally have been reserved for a sweetheart. Typical entries read as follows:

5 March: Visited Condor this afternoon.

6 March: Did not visit Condor today.

7 March: Went out in Condor.

8 March: Visited Condor today.

Other notes in the book relate to conditions on the water: 'Weather – Lousy; Current – Moderate; Wind – Strong, Downstream.'

On Monday 7 May, however, Brian had more momentous news to record. All his skills with the Sten gun would be unnecessary. The entry for the day read quite simply: 'WAR OVER.' Nazi Germany had surrendered unconditionally to the Allies. It was two and a half weeks before Brian's seventeenth birthday.

The following day, Brian decorated his canoe with red, white and blue ribbon, and wrote in the log book: 'I can now travel in Condor without danger of being torpedoed.'

11

The Inheritance

Black sateen corset from the
Langridge Ltd collection

The Inheritance

Brian has in his possession a suitcase which dates from the 1950s. The suitcase is nothing special in and of itself; it's a typical inexpensive piece of luggage of that era. It has traditional corner patches, a dog-tooth pattern on the exterior and a handle made of moulded plastic that mimics sewn leather. The two clasps that hold it shut are never in quite the right position to lock or unlock smoothly, but when they do, they make a satisfying click and what's inside is worth the wait.

The suitcase contains a collection of ladies' underwear, which traces the evolution of female undergarments from the late 1800s through to the time when the manufacture of corsets and bras in England began to decline.

The garments range from exquisite antique corsets to post-war panty girdles and bras. The suitcase is part of the legacy that Brian inherited from his father and grandfather.

The corset at the top of the suitcase is

very handsome, fashioned out of black sateen, with a trim of black and gold ribbon. The estimated date is 1880, according to a label written by Brian's brother Tony.

When the garment is analysed, as a boat-builder might look at a wooden boat, it's possible to discover its secrets. The structure is provided by eighteen bones, a divided busk at the front and lacing at the back. A visual illusion of complexity has been created by the way the garment has been constructed. Firstly, the separate panels of the corset have been sewn together to give it its unique shape. Next, channels, or 'casings', have been sewn onto the exterior of the garment and it is into these that the bones have been inserted. The seams of stitching cross behind these casings and curve gently inwards at the waist to enhance the impression of the desired silhouette.

The lining contrasts dramatically with the black sateen. It is of oatmeal-white coutil, a tightly-woven cotton fabric which has a characteristic herringbone pattern. Every line of black stitching is shown up in reverse, so each channel of boning can be seen as two parallel lines of tiny black dots, rather like tramlines on a snowy landscape. The individual stitches are so tiny it's hard to count them without the aid of a magnifying glass. Each one is perfectly placed.

There are five studs spaced out evenly along the busk at the front of the garment. When getting dressed, the studs would have to be clipped into place first, before the corset could be tightened by means of laces at the back. When removing the corset, the laces would have to be loosened, to enable the studs to be squeezed more firmly into their clasps before they could be released. It's easy to imagine the pain of flesh accidentally pinched. This garment has a spoon busk, curved to provide a more natural fit to the body. Through one layer of fabric, the bones feel smooth and their inherent pliability is evident. The boning is thought to be whalebone, the traditional but notorious material used in corsetry from the late Elizabethan era onwards.

Whalebone was strong, flexible, light and more comfortable for the wearer than some later substitutes. The 'bones' were not taken from the skeletons of whales but from the baleen plates which act as filters inside their mouths. When the supply channel for whalebone dwindled from the 1870s onwards, other materials for boning came into use. Some of these can also be found in Brian's suitcase: thin strips of steel, encased in paper sheaths and now dotted with rust; flattened steel spirals, some tipped with brass at either end; and compressed cardboard, which was sometimes used for cheaper corsets and became more widespread in wartime as other materials grew scarce. Another homespun alternative was feather-boning, in which goose feathers were pressed and stitched together with a herringbone thread. These 'feather bones' could then be inserted into the boning channels.

The corsets in Brian's rare collection include inexpensive as well as luxury items. There are nine corsets in all. One example from 1880 has been labelled: 'A cheap garment, maybe worn in workhouses, charity institutions etc.' It's a reminder that even the poorest women in society used to wear stays, to preserve decency and to provide structure, which the dresses of the time required. Although 'cheap', the garment is nevertheles beautifully made. At the back it rises just above the shoulder-blades and is cut slightly lower at the front, providing a décolletage. The waist comes down to a point. The colour is hard to identify: what might once have been a pale fawn has now been rendered greenish grey by the passage of time. It has no bones – bones would have added extra expense – and the slightly coarser fabric was clearly intended to make the item more durable. Although simple, it is not without adornment; the top of the garment is trimmed with cream lace, through which a narrow ribbon has been fed.

The label on the next garment to emerge from the suitcase seems a contradiction in terms: 'Girl's Health Training Corset', dated 1900. It is pale blue, with magnolia pink stitching. Corsets like these were worn by girls between the ages of ten and twelve. This one has shoulder-straps with bone buttons. There are two buttonholes for each button so that the size could be adjusted as the wearer grew. The stitching, known as 'fanning', was not just for decoration; it also served the purpose of securing the outer edges of the bones. This corset has only six bones and the rest of the structure is provided by softer 'gang cording', for which a length of piped fabric has been sewn into the garment.

One front-laced corset has four dangling suspenders, which carry cumbersome yet ornate buckles an inch wide. It does not look comfortable. Another is designated a 'sports corset'.

The last corset in the suitcase has been given a startling name. Printed on the inside in dark grey ink is 'The GOODWEAR RADIUM (Regd) Unbreakable Rustproof Spiral Steels'. The printed words run along one inside edge of the corset, next to the busk opening, so a woman would see the name every time she put on or removed the corset.

It's a handsome grey corset, trimmed with black lace and ornamented with black fanning. It was created not by Langridge Ltd, but by JD Williams and Co. There were a number of corset manufacturers in the Bristol area and they all knew each other well, which is probably how it found its way into the suitcase.

The suggested date of the garment is

1900 and the name 'Radium' echoes Marie Curie's discovery of the element in 1898. The word 'radium' was in any case widely used to suggest silkiness or opalescence. In the textile industry, it came to signify 'a plain woven fabric made from silk or synthetic yarn with qualities of crispness, drape and sheen'. Later fabrics would be described as 'radium velvet', 'radium poplin', 'radium taffeta' etc. Together with its 'unbreakable rustproof spiral steels' – two very desirable qualities in boning – this corset would have been considered one of the most modern garments of its time.

12

The Reluctant Apprentice

Brian's beloved Ariel Red Hunter

The Reluctant Apprentice

Brian would willingly have gone to war to serve his country, but instead he was taken on in the cutting room of Court Royal Corsets in Bath. The managing director, who had the wonderful name Mr Angel, started him off at one pound per week.

Brian's whole life had been leading up to this moment – his first appointment in a corset factory – but in truth he was a reluctant apprentice. The corsets he helped to make were more modern than those in the suitcase, but many of the principles were the same. The designs made use of many differently-shaped panels that had to be cut according to the grain of the cloth. Brian's job was to fold the cloth, usually a heavy brocade, so that it was ready for cutting with a band knife. Most of the fabric he folded was white, although salmon pink, a colour known as 'tea rose', was also popular.

Brian then gave the cut work to the machinists. Once a section had been stitched, it would be returned to Brian and his colleague, an elderly gentleman who had big calluses on his fingers from using shears all his life. It had to be trimmed before the next section could be sewn, so that the garment would lie smoothly. After all the rough bits had been trimmed off, Brian delivered the half-made corsets to the sewing room to be finished.

He was still living at *Water Row* and his favourite part of the day was riding his Ariel Red Hunter motorcycle to and from work. When he got to work, he had the tantalising views of the River Avon to distract him. From the lavatory, his favourite room in the building, he could see the gorgeous Pulteney Bridge and canoes paddling along without a care in the world. He wanted to be with them.

This less than promising start was followed by a period as trainee manager at Marks & Spencer, working from their head office in Marble Arch. This meant a move to London, which was very exciting. Brian found lodgings at Swiss Cottage and was able to travel to work every day by bus. At night he listened to the radio. The sweet words 'Aqui Radio Andorra' (Here is Radio Andorra) ushered in an evening of music. Now that he was earning money, he vowed that one day he would visit Andorra.

He was placed in a department known rather cryptically as 'T81' – the corsetry department. There he learnt the systems for ordering, allocation and design. His supervisor was a woman named Mrs Ross.

Corsetry was one of the few areas of employment that provided management positions for women at the time. The Corset Guild of Great Britain published a guide, *The Foundationwear Fitter's Handbook,* which offered advice such as this: 'If you are going to be a saleswoman in a foundationwear department, make up your mind to be a good one. Decide straight away that THE TOP is the place for you, and then enjoy the hard work that will get you there.'

There was one young woman working at head office in whom Brian took an immediate interest. He remembers that she had blonde hair and her eyes held an irresistible appeal. He had never had anything to do with girls before, however, and although he took her out a couple of times, no romance ensued.

Soon Brian was working at a number of different branches of Marks & Spencer in London. He was astonished by some of the incidents he witnessed. At Holloway Road two street traders who had been selling watches from a suitcase decided to take advantage of the fact that there were doors both at the front and at the back of the shop. They ran through the store to avoid being caught by the police. The manager heroically tried to block their path and got a black eye for his trouble.

At Slough another manager surprised Brian by showing him several small chicks that had been given sanctuary in the office waste paper basket. Brian was told he shouldn't think there was anything odd about that – they were a present for the manager's wife, naturally.

A few weeks later, there was great commotion as an inventor came in to show off a machine he had designed to cut bread rolls in half and spread them with butter. Brian loved the idea. He imagined happy family scenes, in which picnics were prepared in seconds.

The entire staff gathered round to

watch the demonstration with great excitement, but the inventor (who was talking very fast and was rather red in the face) couldn't get the thing to work and went away humiliated. Brian felt for that man.

At the time, shops had raised counters with an area in the middle where sales assistants could stand and serve customers. On the day that Sir Simon Marks, later Lord Marks, visited the Marble Arch store, Brian was serving on the pyjama counter. He felt that his time had come; perhaps he would win the approval of the Chairman of Marks & Spencer. However, it so happened that Brian was wearing a loud Teddy Boy tie that day and Sir Simon Marks was not impressed.

All too soon, Brian's time in London was over. In May 1946, shortly after his eighteenth birthday, a summons arrived through his front door. It was time for him to begin his National Service.

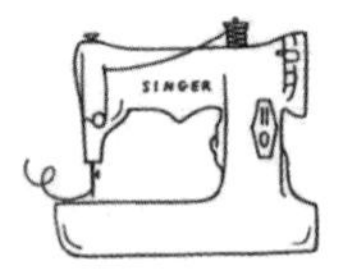
SINGER

13

The Piano Accordion

Brian with his piano accordion

The Piano Accordion

Two months later, Brian was lying on his back in the dust, with his feet up against a fence. To his right and to his left, the other men were doing the same. He closed his eyes against the bright sky. Ten minutes rest in every hour, that was how they did it. Had his uncle Bernard done this in France, he wondered?

He knew instinctively when the ten minutes was up. He was ready for the shout before it came and on his feet again. Another fifty minutes of marching, then another rest, and on until nightfall, maybe longer.

His stomach growled a little. He missed home.

Brian's RAF pass book is so well-worn that it has been buffed to an old gold sheen and the corners are missing. Inside is written in purple ink: 'FLYING CONTROL.' It's the same ink Brian had used for Condor's log book.

'Did you enjoy working at Flying Control?' I ask.

'It was a job.'

'Was it interesting or boring?'

'It was a job. You just went in, did what you had to do and went out. It wasn't like working for yourself.'

Maybe it's significant that the only keepsake he shows me from his National Service days is the book in which he was able to request leave. For time off, he had to detail the date and time he wished his leave to begin, the date and time he would return (usually 23.59, the last minute of the day) and whether or not he was permitted to wear plain clothes (he always was).

Brian's summons for National Service invited him to attend an interview and undergo a medical examination. During the interview he was asked to state his preferences: Army, Navy or Air Force. Dreaming of heroics on a motorbike, Brian said that he would like to be a despatch rider in the Army. He was made a radio telephone operator in the Royal Air Force.

He began his National Service on 2 July 1946. His transport costs were paid to Padgate, Lancashire, where he was issued with an RAF uniform and forage cap and had to hand over his civilian clothes for safekeeping. There he carried out the initial four weeks of basic training: marching on the parade ground and learning how to hold a rifle.

'What was it like?' I ask him.

'Pretty awful.'

'Was it?'

'Yes. The first four weeks were square-bashing. You got shouted at. "Is your cap straight?" That kind of thing. They made you knuckle under. That was the period when the discipline was developed.' Brian pauses and then adds, thoughtfully: 'In the end I found out the sergeant was quite a nice person, when he wasn't on duty.'

Next he was posted to Wilmslow in Cheshire for eight weeks of route marches in the Cheshire countryside. It was on marches like these that he and the other men learnt to ease their aching feet by lying on their backs and putting their feet up.

There he had one unexpected lesson in brutality. On a walk in the woods with another airman, he saw a chick that had fallen from its nest.

Brian was just about to pick it up and put it safely back in the hedge where its mother could feed it, when his companion put the heel of his boot on the chick and killed it.

Life in the Air Force was communal. After a meal, the airmen all washed their knives and forks in a big oil drum filled with hot water outside the dining hall. There were twenty to a dormitory, with ten beds on each side of the room. The men all slept on iron-framed bedsteads with mattresses made up of three rectangular cushions, known as 'biscuits'. The sleeping quarters smelled of polish. This was because every morning the linoleum floor had to be polished until it shone like a mirror. The method for doing this was to pull the 'biscuits' up and down the room with someone sitting on them.

At Wilmslow it was less strict than at Padgate. For one thing, Brian was allowed to have his Ariel Red Hunter with him. The motorbike gave him the freedom to explore the countryside on his own. And, to his delight, he was allowed to return home at weekends. On his first weekend's leave, he turned the bungalow upside down searching for something which he felt sure would transform life at the barracks: his piano accordion. He'd been given it a year earlier by one of his father's friends, a man named Denny Lyons.

Denny worked in a factory in Bristol, but led something of a double life. As well as being a responsible factory employee, he was a talented entertainer and conjuror. During the war, he'd been employed by the Entertainments National Service Association (ENSA) – or, as some people used to say, 'Every Night Something Awful' – to keep up morale. Denny was a source of inspiration for Brian and went on to have a great influence on his life. He was one of the few people who would have understood Brian's impulse to run away and join the circus. He taught Brian a few conjuring tricks and then, one day, handed Brian a piano accordion. He showed Brian the 24 buttons for the left hand and the small piano keys for the right. Brian loved the feel of it in his hands. Before long, he was playing *I'll Be Your Sweetheart* and singing along to it passably well. Denny let Brian keep the piano accordion.

'You're welcome to it,' he said. 'I've got four more!'

When Brian returned to Wilmslow, he

played *I'll Be Your Sweetheart* to the other airmen as they were cleaning the sleeping quarters. He calculated that if he played the accordion well enough, he'd be let off polishing the floor.

From Wilmslow, Brian was sent to Cranwell in Lincolnshire, where he received six weeks of specialised training as a radio telephone operator. It was a welcome change to be doing something other than marching and, when the news came of his subsequent posting, he couldn't believe his luck. He was to be placed at RAF St Eval in Cornwall. It happened to be just a few miles from his parents' holiday bungalow.

At RAF St Eval, Brian worked in Flying Control and was in charge of a squadron of Lancaster bombers. His workplace was a stone building with windows on all sides, and he put his newly-acquired skills into use from day one. St Eval had been of great strategic importance during the war. Just two years earlier, he would have been the first point of contact on land, greeting aircraft on their return from dangerous operations and giving them permission to land. Now it was more mundane. The

Lancaster bombers went out, as before, in search of unidentified submarines, but whereas previously they would have been looking for German U-boats, it was now more a question of the routine policing of British waters and keeping skills sharp.

As soon as Jack learnt that Brian was to be posted to Cornwall, he offered him the key to the bungalow.

'You may as well make use of it. Your mother and I can't,' he'd said. It was true. Petrol was still being rationed, even though the war was over, and Jack didn't have enough spare coupons to make the journey from Bristol. The bungalow had sat untouched for years.

The bungalow was at Trevose Head, approximately four miles from RAF St Eval. One evening, Brian set out to explore it. He turned the key in the lock and pushed open the door. There were a few cobwebs, but it was as if the place had been asleep in the intervening years. He was surprised how clean it was.

He remembered staying there as a boy, and walking from the headland down to Mother Ivey's Bay below, where there was what his mother called 'seashell sand'. She had let it run through her fingers, pointing out the different coloured fragments of shell.

Once he had seen a drowned man floating in the sea between Merope Rocks and the beach, attracting the attention of a flock of seagulls. Brian had been on the cliff and watched as a local farmer, Mr Tummon, swam out and brought the body in to shore. A little later a policeman turned up. Brian remembered the flash of his handcuffs on the back of his belt as he leant over the body. It seemed incongruous. After that somebody wrapped the body in a blanket and it was put on the back of a lorry. The sad story went round that the man had been on his honeymoon in St Ives.

In one of the rooms Brian came across his father's .22 rifle. As he started to clean it, the memories came back to him. His father out on the headland shooting rabbits. The body of a rabbit, glistening and red, with the layer of skin and fur peeled off like a jersey. The strong and surprising taste of rabbit stew. Perhaps Brian could hunt rabbits as well.

Every day Brian went into Flying

Control, where he would be greeted by his colleagues, four WAAFs, who would be seated before he arrived, each at their own desk microphone. The WAAFs ranked as his superiors due to their more extensive experience.

They said: 'Good morning.'

Brian said: 'Good morning.'

That was their conversation for the day. Brian took his place in front of the window. They were ready for the aircraft. The first pilot requested permission to take off. Permission was granted and the plane taxied to the starting point on the runway before take-off. Then with a roar, the bomber lifted into the sky.

This was the daily routine. Always the same. Except today it was different. A curious aeroplane had come into view. It was a Walrus Flying Boat.

At first glance it looked like an ordinary bi-plane, but Brian knew it had a fully retractable under-carriage for touching down on water. He guessed it was from the Fleet Air Arm station at St Merryn. He often got to see unusual aircraft which had set off from there on training missions. Once he had seen a squadron of Seafires coming in, a naval adaptation of the Spitfire. Two or three of them landed and then tipped up on their noses. Brian imagined that the pilots were not used to a hard runway, as at St Merryn they had grass.

After the Walrus Flying Boat landed, Brian noticed it was taxiing up close to Flying Control. Perhaps something was wrong. Concerned, he made an enquiry over the radio to find out what the man wanted. It turned out all he needed was to borrow a spanner!

As soon as Brian was granted a day's leave, he returned to the bungalow and took his father's rifle out onto the head-land. He threw himself down on the scrub-by grass and scanned the landscape for rabbits. Soon one appeared, bobbing along in the late morning sunshine. Brian had shot it before he knew what he'd done. The sound of the shot echoing around the headland startled his companions, two other airmen who were sitting a little way off, smoking cigarettes. A good clean shot. That evening they would have rabbit stew.

Promotion for Brian came when he was least expecting it. He'd earned the designation 'Aircraftman First Class' and was placed in charge of a hut at the top of Bedruthan Steps.

'Have you ever been in charge of a hut?' he likes to say, full of self-deprecation. Brian would receive radio signals from aircraft in flight and give them their bearing using an azimuth compass which had a large aerial on the roof of the hut. Bedruthan Steps, close to St Eval, was and remains a breathtaking location. There is now a National Trust café next to the site where Brian's hut used to be.

It was strange to be in the RAF, but permanently grounded. Brian had not forgotten the airman he'd once seen floating down from the sky. Sometimes he wondered what it would be like to be inside one of the bombers, seeing the world from above. Perhaps he shared this thought once too often, because one day his bluff was called. He was given the chance to fly in a Lancaster bomber.

Brian prepared his kit, albeit with serious misgivings. The flight was to be eight hours long. He knew that temperatures in the sky could drop well below zero. During the war, it had not been unusual for airmen to suffer from frostbite and electrically-heated flying suits had been developed. Brian walked out to meet the waiting aircraft and was about to climb on board, when a glance around the bare metal interior of the Lancaster, criss-crossed with girders, pipes and wires, helped him to make his mind up. He couldn't imagine spending eight hours in there, with barely the space to breathe. He realised with relief that he didn't have to. He turned on his heel and walked away.

So far Brian had done nothing to prove his valour – quite the opposite. The only time he travelled inside an RAF ambulance was when he got something stuck in his eye! A medic rolled his eyelid up on a matchstick and removed the piece of dirt. Brian knew his military career would be nothing to boast of.

That winter, however, he got the chance he was hoping for, the opportunity to be a dashing hero. The winter of 1946-1947 was the harshest European winter for a century. From January to March there was heavy snowfall in Britain, even in Cornwall, where the snow is rarely deep. Having spent much of the summer speeding over the grassy humps of the air raid shelters with his side-car in the air, just for the thrill of it, he was now able to put his motorbike to good use. Brian on his Ariel Red Hunter was the only one able to get through to deliver food supplies from the main base to the hut. His dreams of despatch rider heroism had come true.

When the time came for his final posting, he was naturally reluctant to leave Cornwall. He was to be stationed at RAF Calshot on the Solent in Hampshire, on a shingle spit that protruded out from the coastline opposite the Isle of Wight. The location had been the site of a lookout since the sixteenth century. Calshot Castle was built there by Henry VIII in 1539 as part of his chain of defences along the south coast of England. Not much had changed in the course of four hundred years. Only, back then, the enemies to look out for had been the French and the Spanish.

To begin with, Brian was placed in a rather ordinary hangar halfway along the spit, but after he had been there a couple of months, an electrical fire in the kitchen got out of control and the building burnt down.

To his delight and that of the other airmen, they were relocated to Calshot Castle.

There they carried out a medley of four-hour watches, day and night. They maintained a listening watch on shortwave radio 6440, which was blocked every night by Radio Moscow. They would hear the Russian National Anthem, followed by a programme of Russian music, which Brian loved, with a commentary in both Russian and English. 'A chap came on speaking English and reading the news,' Brian remembers.

On warm nights he and the other airmen took their camp-beds up to the top of the castle and slept out under the stars.

At Calshot, Brian controlled the activities of a squadron of Sunderland Flying Boats. These were amphibious, as the name suggests, and he had to assist them when they took off from or touched down onto water. At night they needed their aqueous 'runway' to be clearly marked.

In order to prepare this for them, Brian and the other airmen travelled out on an RAF launch with rows of dinghies in tow. The dinghies had lights on them, some red, some green. These were secured in lines facing into the wind to make a flare path for the Flying Boats. Once the dinghies were in place, Brian warned all the yachts in the vicinity to keep well away.

In the final summer of Brian's military career, the circus came to town. It wasn't just any circus. It was Bertram Mills Circus. Those performances of the late 1940s still linger in the collective memory as something quite exceptional. The circus had a world-class reputation, attracting the best performers from all over the globe, and Brian didn't want to miss it. He requested leave and drove to nearby Bournemouth in a car he'd been given by his father, a green Vauxhall Velox with silver flukes. He parked it and placed an anchor in front – a visual gag he couldn't resist. In fact it was the anchor from his canoeing days in Condor.

As he made his way into the magnificent circus tent, he could smell sawdust and the sweat of animals. Brian was amazed by what he saw. There were trapeze artists, tumblers, clowns with white-painted faces, a man who put his head inside a tiger's mouth, lions jumping through hoops, troops of horses, elephants playing cricket and performing dogs. He bought a ticket for the next night and the next. He couldn't get enough of it. He wondered if this could be his future. Could he run away and join the circus? In the end he didn't need to because on 2 September 1948 he became a free man again. Brian was demobbed, having carried out his National Service, for, as he likes to say: 'Two years, two months, two days too long.'

14

A Wanderlust

The Vauxhall Velox crosses
The English Channel

A Wanderlust

'If I hadn't had to go to London, I probably wouldn't have met John, and our continental holiday wouldn't have materialised. As it was, I did go to London, I met John, we got talking, and both of us having just recently been demobbed, we decided that we had a wanderlust.'

So begins a typed document on yellowed paper, which reads a little like a story in a popular magazine, but is in fact Brian's account of a spontaneous trip to war-scarred France, Spain and, on Brian's insistence, Andorra. His companion, John Levy, was a handsome and confident young man. It was unusual to travel to the continent so soon after the end of the Second World War, and the sights witnessed by Brian and John were not seen by many.

The adventure began in London. Brian had equipped himself with the necessary 'kit', including a tent, maps and petrol coupons stowed in his trusty four-seater Vauxhall Velox. A delayed crossing meant a change of plan on the very first night.

They were in the tent before they even left English soil, camping on cliffs near Newhaven. They were two young men with nothing to lose and everything to learn.

The next day saw them separated from Brian's precious motor car, which was lifted by crane into a separate boat to be taken across the Channel. In Dieppe, they waited ten hours for the car to be unloaded, again by crane. They could do nothing but watch as several other cars received little knocks and dents. But the Vauxhall emerged unscathed.

Having arrived in France, the first priority was to find lunch. As Brian confesses in his typewritten account: 'Unfortunately, it wasn't going to be as easy as we had thought to order a French meal. To begin with, we couldn't read the writing on the menu, and if we could have, we hadn't sufficiently brushed up our French vocabulary to appreciate what good things were being offered to us.'

Eventually, as he explains, they ended up in the kitchen, with the chef pointing out to them chunks of raw fish and beef. The journey continued with a drive to Chartres, via Dreux.

'At Dreux,' Brian relates, 'we stopped in a typically French square and did something typically French against a typically French lamp-post. And no one took any notice,' he adds, 'which was typically French.'

That night as they lay down in their tent, they chuckled about the owner of the petrol station who had tried to charge them their entire budget for the trip just to put some air in their tyres. They compared notes on the day's successful bartering and wondered sleepily about the monks they'd seen hitch-hiking, with cowls over their heads and rucksacks on their backs, despite the heat.

A few days later, crossing a bridge on the outskirts of Bordeaux at night, they were charmed by what they saw. 'The moon rose above the poplar trees and cast its reflection into the calm waters.'

As they drove further south, they began to think more and more about how good it would be to swim in the sea. And finally they did get a dip.

'At Biarritz we had that swim in the warm surf...'

However, it was to be short-lived. There

was a shrill whistle and they were waved out of the sea by a lifeguard, for reasons they never completely understood.

Back in the car again, two young fellows in a small MG overtook them and gave a gay hoot on their horn as they passed. Brian and John accepted the challenge and raced them through rural villages and up into the mountains. In John's company, Brian lost some of his wide-eyed acceptance of the world. Together they enjoyed their freedom, sometimes in awe of what they saw, sometimes dismissive. They were generous when they could afford to be, but always mindful of their diminishing cash.

At a farmhouse, they managed to communicate their need for water to a six-year-old girl, who showed them to a water pump in the barn. They were very pleased that she understood their French and gave her five francs. But they had nothing to offer the travelling artistes they encountered in a field: two women, a man and three children, performing out of a painted wagon by the light of three bare bulbs, in competition with the hissing and screaming of engines in a nearby shunting yard.

Brian dismissed them as 'rather shoddily dressed and not particularly good'. Perhaps he was still thinking of Bertram Mills Circus. When the clown came round with the hat, the young men hurried away.

They noticed the girls they saw en route, the waitresses with flashing dark eyes and impeccable style, who smiled at their pronunciation. But they admired them from afar, always on the move, checking water, oil, tyre pressure, refuelling constantly, writing their travel journals by torch-light in the tent.

In the Basque country they used a pair of binoculars to admire the local beauties – 'The Basque Belles', as Brian and John called them. They watched the fishing boats coming in and saw the shark-like tuna being taken ashore; one fish was so huge it could hardly be lifted by two grown men. They pitched their tent on a clifftop and fell asleep, lulled by the sound of the surf pounding the cliffs below and, in Brian's words, 'the distant thudding of the Basque boats'. In the morning they were amazed when a van pulled up outside their tent offering them fresh bread.

'What a change,' Brian wrote in his

journal, 'after England.'

And finally they reached Andorra. When they arrived, he was surprised to find that the road between France and Andorra looked as though it was still being built. Andorra seemed no more than a village and Brian noted that the frontier guard was scruffy and unshaven. However, the large white building that housed Radio Andorra was there and that was all he needed to see.

The following year, Brian and John joined forces again and travelled to the Austrian Alps, where they met with misfortune. They pitched their tent in the mountains and went to bed, leaving all their belongings in the Vauxhall Velox. In the morning everything had disappeared. The men had only the clothes they had gone to bed in. No food, no money, no papers. They made a complete inventory of the stolen items and these included a brown leather briefcase containing money and travellers' cheques, 22 units of petrol coupons, ferry tickets and every single one of their official documents. Brian was without passport, Allied Force permit, car registration book, driving licence. And his insurance certificates had gone too. It was an awkward situation to be in.

They walked down to the village where they were greeted kindly, given breakfast for free and introduced to the local policeman, who took them to the nearest town on his motorbike. Brian got to ride pillion, while John travelled in the sidecar. At the police station they explained their predicament. To their immense relief, they were given an official pass and enough money to get back home.

This excellent assistance did not end when Brian returned home. He received a total of six different letters over the course of the next three months. The first, arriving just a week after the incident, informed him that the thief had been apprehended and most of the property recovered. A list of Brian's goods was enclosed with the letter. Items mentioned included a blue and white bathing costume, a Gossen Sixtus camera light meter, a tweed hacking jacket, a ring with a skeleton on it, sketch books, maps and a wallet with cash and travellers' cheques. Almost all the items had been found, but four never were: his British identity card, his British driving licence and – intriguingly – a paper knife and an artificial snakeskin belt. A whole detective novel could be written about what happened to these particular items.

A month after the theft, Brian received a letter to this effect: 'We have packed your property in a clean good wooden case, which we strapped with two iron ribbons.'

The items were delivered to his home in Saltford, cash on delivery.

Whether or not Brian intended to publish his travel memoirs, it is hard to know, but the typed transcript (in duplicate) with the title, *A Search for the Sun*, suggests that this was the case. He seems to have abandoned the idea two pages in, however, no doubt due to other demands on his time. When he returned to England he found his place at last within the family corsetry business.

15

A Pair of Nylon Stockings

Boarding a Silver City aircraft

A Pair of Nylon Stockings

There are some black and white photographs with decorative edges showing the manager of Langridge Ltd, Norman Horler, and Brian's brother Tony holding up two corsets which dwarf them completely. Each one was big enough for three men to step inside. Tony looks as though butter wouldn't melt in his mouth. Mr Horler looks faintly amused. In private, they used to joke about these gigantic corsets, which would be sent to the Netherlands, and refer to their wearers as 'the Dutch stouts'.

Brian started to work for Langridge Ltd in Bristol, which was by now back at the familiar 248a Church Road site. He was in quality control, making use at last of the skills acquired during his apprenticeship at Court Royal Corsets. He had to trim the garments and inspect the seams before packing them in tissue paper, placing them in boxes and sending them down the chute – the same chute he and his brother had slid down many years before.

From the window of the sewing room,

Brian could see when bolts of fabric arrived at the factory. They were delivered on the back of an unusual vehicle, a Great Western Railway Scammell lorry. At the front was a three-wheeled tractor unit, which was brown with a circular GWR logo on the side, and at the back was a fully articulated trailer. The vehicle was thought to be so versatile that it was dubbed 'The Mechanical Horse'.

In the two years Brian had spent on military service, his father had not been idle. While Brian was at RAF St Eval working as a radio telephone operator and shooting rabbits, Jack had been planning the launch of a new factory in Cornwall.

At the time Cornwall was considered a 'depressed area' and there were government incentives to encourage businesses to invest. Jack took advantage of this and in September 1946 he opened a bra factory in Camborne to complement the corset factory in Bristol. There were twelve employees initially and the first cheque for wages came to 40 pounds. It was one of the first factories in the area to employ women. Significantly for Jack, having a business in Cornwall meant he was entitled to extra petrol coupons. He was now able to visit both the factory and the bungalow. Thus, as Brian tells the story, the desire for weekends by the sea led to the establishment of a new bra factory in Camborne.

After Brian had been at Langridge Ltd for six months, he was given a new role – one which he absolutely loved. He got to drive the company van. The bra factory did not have its own cutting room, so cut work bundles were prepared in the Bristol factory and Brian's new job was to transport these to Camborne each week. He drove down every Monday and returned with the finished garments every Friday.

The company van was a modified ex-army truck. The roads to Cornwall were usually empty (indeed, when asked what he misses about the old days, the first thing Brian mentions is the joy of driving on roads with no traffic). Sometimes Brian would break his journey by sleeping outside underneath the truck. He also acquired some favourite places to stay, where he knew he would be well fed. One was a vegetarian guesthouse named *Woodcote,* whose lawns drifted down towards the Hayle estuary. Another was the *Red Lion Hotel* in Truro, which has since been demolished. It dated back to the seventeenth century and Brian used to like its sloping floors.

Eventually the ex-army truck was replaced by a brand new blue van, which was much more comfortable, spacious and fast. Everyone at the factory was proud of it. But one day Brian was driving down an exceptionally steep road, Truro Hill in Penryn, when the van skidded on wet tarmac and crashed into a wall opposite. The vehicle was written off entirely.

Despite such mishaps, Brian became a valued member of his father's firm. In October 1951, when he was twenty-four years old, it was agreed that he would set off with his parents and aunt on an excursion across Europe that would be both a holiday and a business trip. It was to be an epic journey covering a distance of 2,967 miles.

The party would cross sixteen frontiers and reach a height of 4,800 feet on the Simplon Pass. They would set foot in France, Belgium, Holland, Germany, Switzerland, Italy and Luxembourg.

For Brian it was an opportunity to make business contacts in Europe that would serve him in his future career – but he also had a mission of his own.

'Before leaving Bristol,' he confided in a travel journal, 'I was given a pound note by a certain young lady and asked to buy a pair of nylon stockings.'

Jack was to be the sole driver on the trip and Brian's travel journal is suitably deferential. It's a disarming assemblage of cartoonish drawings and rather ambitious flourishes. Brian had clearly been experimenting with calligraphy at the time.

Penned in black ink on carefully ruled lines are the title pages: 'A Ride with Dad by Brian J Sherriff 1951' and on the next page: 'This Book I Dedicate To Dad – who was so kind, and without whom we could not have had such a good time.'

Sketches at the front of the book show him and his father rendered in parallel portraits: broad-shouldered, jacketed, capable. Yet Brian does not shy away from poking fun at his father, showing him as bald with a single hair springing up on the top of his head and over-long legs, which run over the edge of the page and are continued in an additional sketch. These were the legs that would operate the accelerator and clutch and drive them all over Europe. The fact that Brian was actually taller than his father by this time isn't reflected in the pictures.

Brian's mother Joan also features in the sketches. She appears well-dressed but rather flustered, and aunt Marie, whom Brian always describes as 'jolly and rotund' (and of whom he was very fond), is faithfully rendered. Both the ladies carry handbags and everyone has fingers like bunches of sausages.

Two nights before their departure, Brian was staying at his favoured *Red Lion Hotel* in Truro. He opened the sketchbook which was to be his travel journal in the hotel lounge and wrote: 'As I was motoring down here today, it occurred to me that at the moment I know very little more of what will fill the pages of this book than the reader.' There is the sense that he is on the cusp of a new adventure; his whole life, not just a trip to mainland Europe, is ahead of him.

Between midnight and 2 am on 26 October the results of the British General

Election came through on television. Brian recorded, with a sense of drama: '2.30 am. I lay my weary body to rest.'

The following day, Brian collected his Aunt Marie and the entire party travelled to Ashford in Kent, where they spent the night. On Saturday 27 October their journey began.

'Up bright and early. Breakfast at 8.45, Lympne Airport at 9.20, airborne at 9.55, landed 10.15 and on the road at 10.30 am. Such was the rapid way of things that memorable morning.'

Brian included a sketch of his dad's car disappearing inside a Silver City aircraft bound for Le Touquet in northern France. At that time it was possible for travellers to take their own cars with them on the plane. The heady tone of Brian's account is quickly undercut, as he relates his experiences before boarding the plane: 'I was questioned twice whilst searching for the toilet at the aerodrome.'

The results of the election were ever-present as they travelled through continental Europe.

'The weather all day was beautiful. It must be the new government,' Brian wrote. The little party was frequently reminded that Winston Churchill had won the election. 'At the frontier an Italian guard was very thrilled to tell us that Churchill was again premier of England.' And later, 'We met a German guard, who was also proud to tell us the news when we crossed into Germany from Holland.'

The progression of Brian's career and private life had been subjected to an unnatural pause by National Service. Now he wanted to make up for lost time. In Antwerp he was dazzled by glimpses of the high life.

'I wandered by myself along the brightly lighted streets,' he wrote. 'I joined a crowd and watched some big cars drawing up outside a large and palatial building and saw several people set out, wearing evening dress, cross the pavement and disappear in the hall swarming with butlers and door keepers and many other uniformed people. I wished I had an evening dress and fair partner so that I could join in and see what it was about!'

Brian did not know it at the time, but he would soon be retracing his steps, exploring Europe not in the company of his family, but with a new bride.

Brian saw poverty and wealth, simplicity and sophistication. And there were sobering reminders. On the Menin Gate in Ypres he saw the names of all the men killed in the surrounding area whose bodies were never found.

He saw 'horribly damaged' German towns and travelled along an Autobahn full of potholes. It was slow going, with an average speed of no more than 40 miles per hour. In some districts it was as if time had stood still for centuries. He saw peasants picking grapes along the Rhine and carrying them in baskets on their backs to carts towed by bullocks. One plough-girl asked him to take a photograph of her and her companions. He jotted down the address to send it on to her later.

Food was a constant preoccupation. There was still rationing in England and, whilst visiting the German city of Mainz, Brian noted wryly: 'I went around the shops of the conquered race and saw many things that are unobtainable in England at very reasonable prices: ham – as much as you like 10d for a pound. Sultanas, cheese, chocolate and sweets, clothing and overcoats cheaper than in England, and also corduroy trousers (made in Manchester) £2.10 or the equivalent.'

In the Black Forest, Brian went out alone one morning, before the rest of his family was up, to see the Triberg waterfall. It was a rare moment of solitude.

And finally he accomplished the mission entrusted to him. In Amsterdam he purchased stockings for the young woman back in England. Nor was his business acumen wasted in the transaction.

'I bought three pairs for a little over £1, and with every three pairs one gets one pair free, so that certain young lady will be very lucky it seems.'

16

Sheriff Bryan and his Square Dance Posse

Sheriff Bryan and his Square Dance Posse
– the arch is formed by Pat and Brian

Sheriff Bryan and his Square Dance Posse

Brian, his parents and Aunt Marie returned to England on 10 November 1951. The whole trip had lasted only two weeks. Brian lost no time in delivering the stockings. The recipient was Heidi Loeff, whom Brian had taken out a couple of times on his motorbike. She was a nurse and worked at a health home in Bristol owned by Brian's aunt Dorothy. Perhaps Heidi was amused that the stockings had come from the Netherlands, as she was herself Dutch. Heidi may have been the recipient of the four pairs of nylon stockings, all for the bargain price of just over one pound, but she was not the woman destined to be his wife. That role, however, was soon to be taken.

In *Picture Post,* a society magazine popular in the 1950s, a photograph appeared of a fresh-faced Brian in evening dress sitting next to a young woman in a diaphanous gown at the Assembly Ball in Bath. The expression on his face is open and eager, an attitude that was to remain with him all his life. The beautiful woman at his side looks, quite simply, happy.

'This is where my life started,' Brian says, looking at the photograph 65 years later.

In 1952 Brian enrolled at Bath Technical College to learn Spanish, a decision that was to have a singularly positive effect on his life. On the first day, as he was waiting for the class to begin, he started to unwrap a bar of Cadbury's Dairy Milk chocolate. Reflecting that it would be rude not to offer some to the girl sitting next to him, he did so. She accepted and after that, as he puts it, he 'had to marry her'.

The girl at the Spanish class was Patricia Harvey. She had long dark hair and a beautiful smile. Brian later described her as 'strong and capable, with an excellent sense of humour'. The two were so delighted to have met each other that neither of them ended up learning much Spanish.

Patricia worked at a solicitors' office in Bristol and Brian asked if he could take her out after work. She agreed. So every Friday at five o'clock, Brian parked at the corner of the road on which she worked and waited for his first glimpse of her. They went for drives and picnics in the countryside and soon discovered a new passion – square dancing.

Perhaps what was most remarkable about their meeting was the fact that they lived within half a mile of each other in Saltford. They had been living parallel lives for years. Patricia, who was usually known as Pat, lived in The Shallows and Brian lived in Mead Lane. They had never met as children and in recent years their paths had not crossed because Pat always travelled to work by bus, whereas Brian drove into Bristol by car.

For some time Brian had been curious about his surname. The word 'sheriff' derives from the Old English 'scírgeréfa', which literally means 'shire-reeve'. Before the Norman Conquest, a sheriff in England was a high officer, the representative of royal authority in a shire, a man responsible for the execution of the law. As a surname, almost every conceivable variation in spelling exists. As a family name, it couldn't have been more appropriate.

Brian's ancestors include three generations of prison governors, who presided over Aylesbury Gaol from the eighteenth century well into the nineteenth century. Brian's great great great grandfather Henry was appointed gaol-keeper of Aylesbury County Gaol in 1788. He was followed in this office by his son James and grandson Henry, meaning that there was a period of approximately 90 years during which a Sherriff was the governor of Aylesbury County Gaol.

Brian felt he could not let a good surname go to waste. Riding the wave of love for all things American that followed the end of the Second World War, he set about teaching himself square dancing from a book. Shortly afterwards, 'Sheriff Bryan and his Square Dance Posse' was unleashed onto a more-than-willing public. The group offered their services regularly at *The Old Mill* in Bath and also performed at events such as meetings of Young Conservatives, Rotary Club and village fetes.

Sheriff Bryan – he assumed a different spelling of his name for the role – acted as caller and his 'posse' of four couples would put on a display, showcasing the best dances to an admiring audience or leading the public in a hoe-down.

Pat was always there, arriving in her small Triumph Herald, the leading light of the display team. She was very welcoming to newcomers, sharing her smile with everyone and encouraging men and women of all ages to dance. She also provided practical help, running up the girls' dresses and the men's shirts on her sewing machine. The girls wore gingham frocks and bonnets that tied under the chin. The boys got to dress up as cowboys. Their Stetsons were donated by Dunn's, a local hat retailer. Brian had a cap pistol and his costume included a neck-tie, a belt which looped around his thigh (to stop his pistol and holster flapping about), cowboy boots and – of course – a sheriff's star. He also wore his aunt Gladys' famous leather wrist gauntlets from Guyana.

Sheriff Bryan and his Square Dance Posse performed with a number of local bands. Their regular band was The Deputies Square Dance Band, but they also enjoyed music from the rather geekily named Set Square Band made up of students from Bristol Architectural College. Members of the band used to dress up in checked shirts and boasted an impressive range of instruments: fiddle, clarinet, accordion, drums, double-bass and piano.

The local papers were full of advertisements for the Square Dance Posse and exhortations to 'rustle up your pards and join the fun!' – with additional comments such as, 'Yippee! It sure is mighty fine!' On one page of the *Bath and Wilts Chronicle and Herald,* the square dancers were announced alongside a column of cinema listings. Rival attractions on one week in June 1952 were: *Inside the Walls of Folsom Prison,* Humphrey Bogart in *Murder Inc,* Kirk Douglas and Eve Miller in *The Big Trees* and Loretta Young in *The Silent Voice*.

Brian Sherriff and Betty Patricia Harvey were married at Saltford Church on 20 December 1952. As Brian drove his new bride to the reception at *The Glen* in Bristol, he was stopped by a policeman, who was directing traffic from a pedestal in the middle of the road. The policeman told him off for wearing a top hat and for looking so happy!

17

Featherwhite

Pat Sherriff during the
'Honeymoon on Ice'

Featherwhite

The couple had been married a mere four days when, on Christmas Eve, they found themselves in a snowy wood in Switzerland without a bed for the night. They slept in Brian's Austin A40, with the snow drifting all around them, and somehow managed to keep each other warm.

By this point, Pat must have known that life with Brian would never be dull. Brian's journal, *Honeymoon on Ice,* describes the couple's 2,050 mile road-trip across Europe. It sometimes reads like an extract from the first James Bond novel, *Casino Royale,* which would come out the following year.

'We had several exciting moments when we met other cars and had to pass with a precipice up one side and sheer down on the other!' Brian noted in the diary. He was characteristically nonchalant.

'We found that hard snow or ice was quite alright for safe driving,' he added. 'We often touched 60-70 miles per hour on it, but care was necessary on corners. Only once did we prang – on a hairpin bend in the Alps, and that was through going too slowly.'

On Christmas morning, the weary lovers checked into the Zurich Hotel and did not emerge until the middle of the next day. On rising and finding everything closed and a mysterious note left on their car door: 'Bitte telefonieren' ('Please telephone'), they did as they were bid. A single call established that only one pass was open over the mountains, the Julier Pass. Undaunted, they got into the car and continued on their way.

'The road was deep in snow, lakes were frozen and it was too cold for trees.'

On the road up to Arosa, the car wheels started to spin on the icy surface and Brian asked Pat to get out and push. The vehicle started to move forward and Brian continued to drive, leaving Pat stranded. He needed to keep the momentum going so that the vehicle would be able to make it up the slope. However, it was dark and bitterly cold outside the car and Pat thought she had been left behind. She walked as fast as she could to catch up with him and when she got into the car she was very angry with him.

A week later they arrived in Paris.

'Still plenty of snow,' he wrote, 'but a very quiet Paris on New Year's Day.' They drank in the New Year with tomato juice.

On returning home, Brian and Pat bought half an acre of land. This was where they would construct their dream home. They moved into a caravan, from which they were able to see their house gradually take shape, a bungalow of Brian's design. The work began in February.

It was a cold time of year to be in a caravan, but it was nothing compared to the Christmas Eve they had spent together in the Alps. The land at South Tehidy near Camborne was cleared by means of a tractor.

The foundations were laid and Brian took a keen interest in the construction process, documenting every stage. When the external walls went up he paced on top of them and helped to fit Canadian cedar wood shingles onto the roof. He took some rather vertiginous photographs while he was up there.

Brian had not forgotten the spiritualist meetings he'd attended with his parents and once the bungalow was completed, he decided to name it after his spirit guide, White Feather. But he reversed the words, giving the bungalow the unusual and attractive name, *Featherwhite*.

Even after the move to Cornwall, Brian and Pat continued to spread the excitement of square dancing, travelling long distances to attend events. The proceeds of their performances usually went to charity. One grateful thank you letter after an event is effusive, stating: 'For Mrs Sherriff and yourself to have travelled all the way from Cornwall just to help us, and to have shown such generosity in addition, we find it hard to find suitable words of thanks.'

Sadly, Brian and Pat were unable to find as much enthusiasm for square dancing in Cornwall as they had found in Bristol and Bath. Finally Sheriff Bryan and his Square Dance Posse kicked off their cowboy boots and hung up their Stetsons and bonnets for the last time.

Winter arrived and there was snow in Cornwall. Brian and Pat were glad to be in their snug bungalow and not in the caravan, not least because they were now expecting their first child.

18

The Bra-kerchief

The presentation card for
Brian's Bra-kerchief

The Bra-kerchief

When the time for the birth drew nearer, not one, but two doctors were called to the house. Brian's task was to go to the kitchen and boil some water so that the equipment could be sterilised. Unfortunately, in his excitement he failed in his one simple assignment. The hot water never materialised. Nevertheless, a daughter, Belinda Anne, was welcomed into the world to the delight of her parents.

When Brian was appointed director of Langridge Ltd in Camborne, the brassieres being produced still carried whispers of an age of elegance. One popular bra was made from satin in the colour known as 'tea rose'. The straps were made from ribbons similar to those you might find on a ballet shoe. This delicacy and style belonged to a vanishing era.

Modernity would soon be ushered in, with fabrics such as nylon and spandex and the awkwardly-named 'power lace'. In his father's factory, corsets were also changing. No longer referred to as stays, the figure-enhancing under-garments of the 1950s and 1960s came to be known collectively as 'foundation-wear' and individually by names such as 'power net girdle'. But most importantly the bra had finally come into its own.

Brian acquired twenty-five shares in Langridge Ltd at £10 each and took over the directorship of the Camborne factory. It was a big step for him and at first he wore his authority with diffidence. He had metal tips attached to the heels of his shoes so that anyone would be given fair warning as he approached. He did not want to catch anyone doing anything they shouldn't. One of his early employees, Sandra Vincent, recalled that he was a forbidding figure approaching in his dark suit with the clip-clop sound of his shoes as he walked down the factory floor.

As was customary for the era, all employees at the factory received a small guidebook, which was at once many things: an introduction to the company, a motivational 'tonic' and a list of rules. *An Introduction to Your Work with Langridge Ltd* was a tiny book, about the size of a playing card, with a pale pink cover. It was seven pages long. The hourly rates of pay were listed within it. The machinists were started off at a basic rate and then went on to piece work. The book contained wholesome affirmations, such as 'good work means good wages' and 'a good garment will please a customer, but a bad garment will lose a customer'. The message could not be disputed, but Brian managed to bring something new to the factory. To the solid work ethic and worthy ideals, he added a sense of fun and inclusive good will.

Brian wanted the factory to be a happy place to work. As the machinists were paid for what they did, rather than the hours they worked, they had an incentive to work quickly and accurately and this led to a sense of satisfaction in what they could achieve. At a public event to promote the factory and recruit new employees, one machinist demonstrated that she could make a complete bra in thirteen minutes.

Brian has an album of photographs from the factory, and the way in which the names of the various employees have been recorded under each picture bears witness to a degree of care and affection. For example, there is Reggie Roach demonstrating the band knife, with a note in the caption underneath the photograph stating that he was an ex-miner. There is Margaret Rogers, the cutter, pictured operating the double-geared press. This piece of apparatus was a source of pride at Langridge's; it could cut 100 pieces at a time. Mrs Mounce, the cleaner and canteen worker, can be seen perching with a shy smile behind a sewing machine to have her picture taken.

It was springtime and Brian was once again pacing the rooms of *Featherwhite* in nervous anticipation. Pat was expecting the birth of their second child. The midwife, Nurse Perkins, had arrived, but there was no sign of the doctor.

This time Brian could not hide in the kitchen. He was needed to help with the birth. As the expectant parents and midwife waited anxiously for the baby to be born, the gardener stuck his head through the window and said to Pat: 'Want a pasty, ma'am?' A pasty was very far from her thoughts at that moment.

Finally, with the aid of neither pasty nor

doctor, Brian's second daughter, Susan Angela, was delivered safely into the world.

Every form of transport was exciting to Brian, but he had never flown a plane. After the birth of his second daughter, he decided it was time to change that. He reasoned that he travelled to London regularly for meetings with wholesalers and it would be quicker to fly than travel by train; it would be a practical, not to say exciting, mode of transport.

Although Brian had carried out his National Service in the RAF, his career had been exclusively on terra firma. His one opportunity to travel in a Lancaster bomber had been passed up. Nevertheless, almost ten years after completing National Service, he acquired a student pilot's licence, valid for two years, and started to take flying lessons at Plymouth Aero Club in a Tiger Moth bi-plane. It was a dream come true – in theory at least. During one memorable flight he was sick over the picturesque village of Chagford in Devon. He decided flying wasn't for him.

Brian was happier on land – and on water. Over time he was the proud owner of a series of boats, of which his favourite was Donghadee. Once he, Pat and their two daughters delivered a consignment of bras to Marks & Spencer in Falmouth by boat. The two girls looked very smart in their sailing caps as Donghadee pulled up alongside the back entrance of Marks & Spencer on the Fal Estuary.

Part of Brian's role was to visit wholesalers, discuss existing orders and gain new commissions. For this, he had developed a unique calling card. Like most gentlemen at the time, he wore a handkerchief in his top pocket, with just the starched peaks showing. But in Brian's case, it wasn't an ordinary handkerchief. Although he never made it into the circus, he still had something of the showman about him. He had learnt a few conjuring tricks, and in a way this was one of them. When Brian took a handkerchief out of his top pocket at business conferences or dull meetings, he got everybody's attention because it wasn't a handkerchief at all, but a beautifully crafted miniature bra. The Bra-kerchief, as he called it, proved to have widespread appeal. It even had its own presentation pack which read: 'Size 15 inch. Guaranteed to fit ... as long as you're the right size!'

Soon more space was needed at the factory. By 1959 there were seventy machinists at Langridge Ltd, Camborne, producing 500 dozen brassieres per week, and by 1960 staff numbers had risen to one hundred. The plan to bring more employment to Cornwall was working. The factory had already expanded into the Old Fire Station adjoining the Old Council Offices and later the Magistrates Hall. Langridge Ltd opened a new cutting department nearby, but even so they needed more space.

It was time for a brand new, purpose-built factory. A suitable site was identified, on Vean Road in Camborne, and Brian was given carte blanche to develop it as he wished. The new factory, he decided, would be light and spacious, with windows all down one side of the sewing room. The toilet cubicles and hand basins had to be completely up-to-date. For the floor, Brian chose a tartan pattern, very much in vogue, and for the canteen, black and white tiles. He decided that the walls would be painted in bright colours: magnolia, coral and green.

On the day of the official opening, Brian was flanked by three generations of his family. His parents were in any case company directors and his brother Tony was the sales director. His two daughters seemed alternately intrigued and bored by the proceedings. The Mayor of Camborne was in attendance and the local MP, David Price, cut the ribbon – a bra-strap! On 3 October 1962 the factory was declared open.

It was here, in this new factory, that Brian decided to launch his own clothing labels, Secret Charm and Malibu (written with a star on the letter 'i'). Some of the machinists modelled the swimwear and beachwear and the resulting photographs were used in glossy promotional brochures.

There is one black and white photograph of three bathing beauties, which has clearly been staged in an office room. A brunette lounges at the front on a piece of fabric with a sunhat across her knees. Her luscious, shoulder-length hair flicks out and she wears the heavy eye make-up and nude lipstick of the 1960s. Her swimsuit is of a daring design with cut-away flanks. The young woman gazes wistfully into the middle-distance and it is to her that one's eyes are first drawn. The composition is as balanced as any Renaissance painting of *The Three Graces*. Counterbalancing the recumbent woman is another dark-haired lady who stands with her hands lightly placed on her thighs. One leg is slightly raised, perhaps placed on a block just out of view. Maintaining the illusion of a beach scene (which comes across despite the tell-tale electrical sockets that can be glimpsed on the wall behind), a third young woman stands in a bikini, toying with a pair of sunglasses. Her swimsuit is of wet-look fabric and her hair is in an up-do, decorated with a leopard-print headscarf.

Pat's natural talent lay in design and, after her children had been born, she began to create garments at Langridge Ltd for well-known chain stores and swimsuits for Jantzen. Her items of swimwear and beachwear proved very popular. Before long, the new label Secret Charm was doing very well, with garments selling in Bermuda, the Near East, Malta and Sweden.

However, the sight of Pat on the factory floor one day incurred the disapproval of her mother-in-law, who held the opinion that it was not appropriate for the wife of the director to work, and certainly not within the factory. The rift that followed the chance meeting of the two women lasted many years, until Brian and Pat decided it was easiest simply not to mention the fact that Pat was working for the business.

19

Twelve Stitches Per Inch

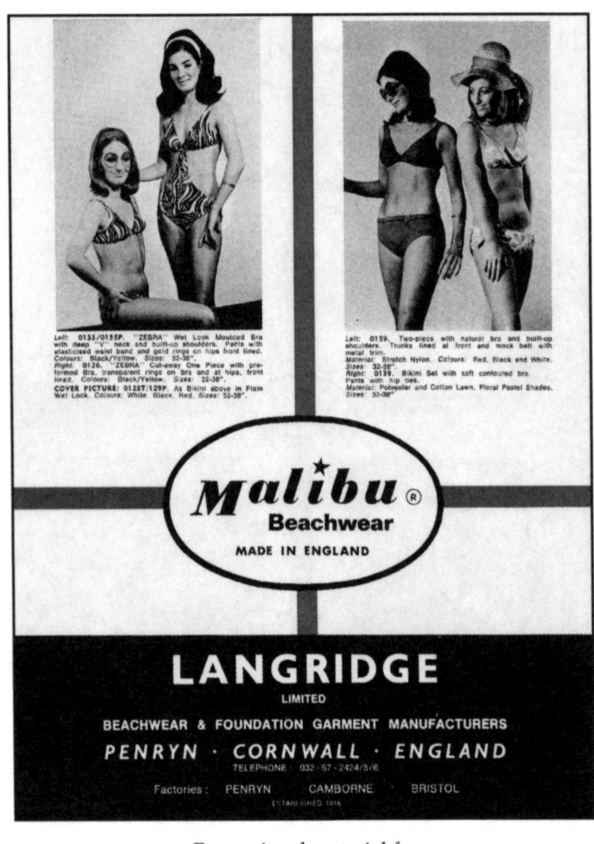

Promotional material for
Brian's beachwear label

Twelve Stitches Per Inch

In September 1965 an article in *The West Briton* announced: 'Girls at Langridge's Camborne factory work on piece-rates and take home an average pay packet of nearly £9 a week.' It's the comment following this that gives pause: 'In some cases as much as their fathers earn.'

A talented machinist had the possibility not only of increasing her wages by fast, accurate work, but also of gaining promotion to the role of supervisor, senior supervisor or manager. It was possible to build up a respectable career for oneself.

One machinist who benefitted from the opportunities offered by Langridge Ltd was Jean Wills, née Tenby. There's a photograph of Jean standing in front of a group of her colleagues looking straight into the camera and smiling. The picture was taken at the Camborne factory in 1960. She is wearing a long-sleeved dress and looks about seventeen years old, a fresh-faced Pippi Longstocking, although in fact she was just shy of twenty. As the caption below the photograph indicates, she was soon to be married and promoted to the position of supervisor.

When Jean started working at the factory at the age of fifteen she was a complete novice, straight out of school. She had never used a sewing machine before. As she explained in an interview at her home in Cornwall: 'In those days my mother couldn't afford a sewing machine.' She went through the induction procedures for new staff and gained a thorough training in how to use the machines. In the next five years she learnt how to operate all of them: the overlocker, the straight stitch and a special machine for stitching the undercups of bras.

Brian had developed an innovative training method, together with his production engineer, Robert Griffiths, to assist a machinist in learning new techniques. Firstly, a more experienced machinist was filmed carrying out a job correctly. The camera was carefully positioned so that it would show the viewpoint of the machinist. This film was then projected onto a small screen in front of the sewing machine of a less experienced seamstress. It was played on a loop – the strip of 8mm film was literally cut and taped together so that it would run and run. In this way, the machinist could look from her own work to the example being projected just in front of her, make comparisons and hone her technique.

Langridge Ltd made bras for Marks & Spencer, Evans Outsize, British Home Stores and Littlewoods. They made bras from size 28 to size 46 bust. Of the largest bras, Jean commented: 'They were massive. They were like hammocks, in my eyes!'

The Marks & Spencer bras had to be sewn with twelve stitches per inch.

'They had to be perfect,' she said, 'and I mean perfect.'

If a mistake was made, it was possible to unpick it and start again, but if a complete garment had been made with, say, ten stitches per inch or fourteen stitches per inch, then the label was cut out and it would be sold off elsewhere as flawed stock. Jean had nothing but admiration for her firm-but-fair supervisor, Sylvia Bassett, who later became a manager.

The factory hours were 8am to 5pm, with half an hour off for lunch. Lunches were made by Olive in the canteen.

'Everybody loved her,' Jean says. 'She was the best scrambled egg person.' Olive's speciality was scrambled egg sandwiches.

Some of the employees had lunch in the canteen, which had to be ordered first thing in the morning. Others brought food in from home or went out into town, as the factory was right in the centre of Camborne. Jean chose to work on Saturday mornings, and for this she received overtime pay. She said: 'The more you produced, the more money you got. At the end of the day it was well worth it. It gave me a good standard of living.'

Jean's main task was sewing hooks and eyes onto the back elastics of bras. Everyone worked on one specific part of a bra, which was later incorporated into an entire garment. Some of the machinists also helped with the fitting of the garments.

Jean's 'hourglass' figure, 36-24-36, made her an ideal candidate for this. Mrs Bassett would often ask her to try on bras and bikinis to make sure they were a good fit. On some days Jean would be constantly getting dressed and undressed.

Jean made it her business to understand the factory inside out. She wanted to know how a sewing machine was put together, so that if the mechanic were ill or on holiday, she would be able to fix it and carry on with her work. After five years at the factory, Jean was promoted to supervisor.

'It boosted me,' she says. 'It gave me confidence.'

Not all the women employed in the factory were Cornish. In Jean's team there was a Spanish woman, an Italian woman from Sicily and a South African woman. Jean's Cornish accent proved something of a challenge; she had to remember to speak slowly. Referring to her international team she says: 'They made fantastic machinists. They worked by the rules and the books.' The Italian woman also made wedding dresses as a sideline.

But it wasn't always easy being a supervisor. It was up to Jean to enforce the 'twelve stitches per inch' rule. Women of all ages worked at the factory and some did not take kindly to being told what to do, especially not by a relative youngster.

For all that, it was an enjoyable place to work and not too strict. There were social events. There was the Christmas party. Pin-ups of matinee idols, if not actively encouraged, were at least tolerated; some of these were taped to the wall near the inspection table and some were even affixed ingeniously to sewing machines. As in the Bristol factory, the machinists listened to music on the radio, which played softly in the background. To begin with this was *Music While You Work*, half an hour in the morning and half an hour in the afternoon. Later, they listened to the radio all day.

The factory even had a visit from the actor who played Dan Archer in the BBC radio series *The Archers*. And once Jean was herself invited to be on the radio, along with a colleague named Ethel. They were apparently chosen on account of their broad Cornish accents.

Factory banter was inevitable. Jean's fiancé was employed at Holman's No. 1 Works, the factory across the road. When the couple got married within twelve months of meeting, everybody said she must be pregnant. In fact it was another ten years before she had her first child. She made sure she pointed this out to her colleagues when the time came.

Although Brian was not in the factory every day – 'he used to flit in and out' – Jean got to know him and Pat well over the years. She also saw Mr Sherriff senior on occasion and remembers that Brian was taller than his father.

'His father was a nice gentleman,' she observes. 'They were both nice gentlemen.'

Jean was very fond of Pat also. They worked closely together on a number of garments. Pat would carry out the design and prepare the fabric and Jean would stitch it for her. In fact, when Pat came to make her first prototype of the beekeeping hood, or 'headgear' as Jean refers to it, it was Jean who stitched it.

When Jean was twenty-two years old, her mother died. Jean was devastated. Life suddenly became very hard for her.

She was grieving, she had a full-time job and overnight she had become the main caregiver in her family. As she put it: 'I had my husband, I had a fourteen-year-old brother to look after and I had my father.'

Brian allowed Jean to go part-time for six months.

'That's kindness itself,' Jean says. 'You appreciate all these things and you don't forget them.'

When Jean decided it was time to leave the factory and start a family, it was not without regrets. Brian showed his kindness once again. He and Pat gave her a silver spoon and a knife with a pearl handle to thank her for all her work. When Jean's daughter was born, Brian wrote to her.

No sooner had Jean left Langridge's than she was approached by another local factory offering her work. She told them quite categorically that if she had been going to work for anyone it would have been for Brian Sherriff.

20

Fighting for Survival

The bra factory in Camborne

Fighting for Survival

Bees entered Brian Sherriff's life when he needed them most, and the decisive moment came during a visit to the Royal Cornwall Show. Brian and Pat had already visited the dog tent, the pigeon tent and the rabbit tent. But when they entered the bee tent, something felt different. Brian smelt the beeswax and cedar wood and saw the queen in the observation hive and he somehow knew beekeeping was for him.

Laid out on the table were rows upon rows of competition honey. He knew nothing at all about bees at that time, but he knew that his family ate a lot of honey. He left with two empty beehives and the next day the bees arrived, ushering a change into his life he could not, at the time, foresee.

Both colonies of bees died out that winter; he had a lot to learn. Undeterred, he bought seventeen classic white WBC (William Broughton Carr) hives the following year from a man who was giving up beekeeping. This time the hives were successful. Brian needed no further persuasion. He decided to invest in beekeeping in a big way.

It was at about this time that he became friends with George Tonkin, a commercial bee farmer based near Tiverton in Devon, and Athole Kirkwood of the Heather Hills Honey Farm in Perthshire, Scotland. It was George Tonkin who gave him the advice he needed to get set up in business as a bee farmer. Brian bought 400 hives from Heather Hills Honey Farm. The hives were all Smith hives, suited to the Scottish heather moors. Brian felt that they would also be appropriate for the wide open spaces of Cornwall. Smith hives are similar to the British National Hive, although they have a slightly smaller body. The frames inside are the usual size, but they have shorter lugs, or handles.

Under George Tonkin's guidance, Brian invested in commercial bee-farming equipment: feeders, an extractor fan and a tank with an impeller and feeding unit. The tank held 100 gallons of syrup and had a tap at the base for releasing the syrup into plastic buckets or tins, ready to pour into the Smith feeders. The feeders could be positioned on top of each hive in the apiaries.

Brian hired out some of his bees to farms in need of assistance with pollination. Some went to a farmer who grew cauliflowers from seed and some to a grower who had 400 strawberry plants within greenhouses. Before providing the hives, Brian went through a careful procedure, known as 'bleeding', to ensure that only young bees were present in the hives, as these would not sting.

The procedure works by sleight of hand and is reminiscent of the 'cups and balls trick' in conjuring. Two hives are used. The more mature bees are tricked into leaving their original hive, which is moved a little each day without them noticing, and settling in a new hive, which has been placed in the original position of the first hive. Once the original hive has lost all its mature bees and contains only a queen, eggs and young bees, it is ready to be used, for example, in a greenhouse.

Brian's expertise and his fascination for the habits of bees was to stay with him all his life. He would later become quite an authority on beekeeping around the world.

But it soon became evident that Brian's most significant contribution to the bee-keeping community would take another form.

The height of success at Langridge Ltd in Camborne had been in the early 1960s. Business had been good, the factory had had its full complement of staff, and garments were produced to extremely high specifications. However, just as Brian had established his successful new factory on the Vean Road premises, market forces changed. The cost of raw materials started to rise. Wholesalers were tempted by cheaper manufacturing overseas and Langridge Ltd lost sales.

The early promise of the labels Secret Charm and Malibu was not fulfilled. On 14 January 1971, an article appeared in *The West Briton* with the headline, 'Firm Fights For Survival'. The firm in question was Langridge Ltd. There was not enough capital to keep the business going. A receiver-manager was called in. Brian pledged that his remaining staff would be kept on for as long as possible and assisted in finding alternative employment. He had nothing but praise for his employees and made it clear that the quality of their work had never been in doubt.

Langridge Ltd was still in business – just – with an order for tracksuits from a surf lifeguard club in Australia and a contract from the British Ministry of Defence to make RAF battledress blouses and sailors' collars with blue and white binding. Brian met each of the RAF recruits personally and measured them up for a uniform. It was a tight deadline. The uniforms had to be ready for marching out on parade four weeks later. He also produced tropical dress uniforms for naval officers. These made use of real gold brocade, which had to be kept in the factory safe.

For all this, Brian's income had dwindled and continued to dwindle. Pat gained employment as a PA to the architect of Carrick Council. Brian had his bees and he was also a member of an industrial tribunal, for which he received some payment, but the situation was unsustainable. He sold his Humber Pullman and acquired a two-seater Fiat 500. He did what he could to economise.

Thinking back to this period of his life,

Brian says: 'I was on my beam ends.' The expression just slips out – it had been a desperate time. The most difficult part was to contemplate what had become of his grandfather's legacy; he had been given so much and to lose it all was hard to accept.

The demise of the business was not instantaneous. Factory work continued in a few different configurations and locations before it ceased completely. There was a collaboration with Mr Bernard of CH Bernard. There was a move to Wilson Way in Pool, near Redruth, followed by a move back to the original factory premises at the Old Council Offices in Camborne. Finally, though, the enterprise which Edgar Sherriff had bought in the late 1800s, which had been passed down to his youngest son Jack and which Jack in turn had passed down to Brian, was no more. And yet, all was not lost.

21

The Bras and the Bees

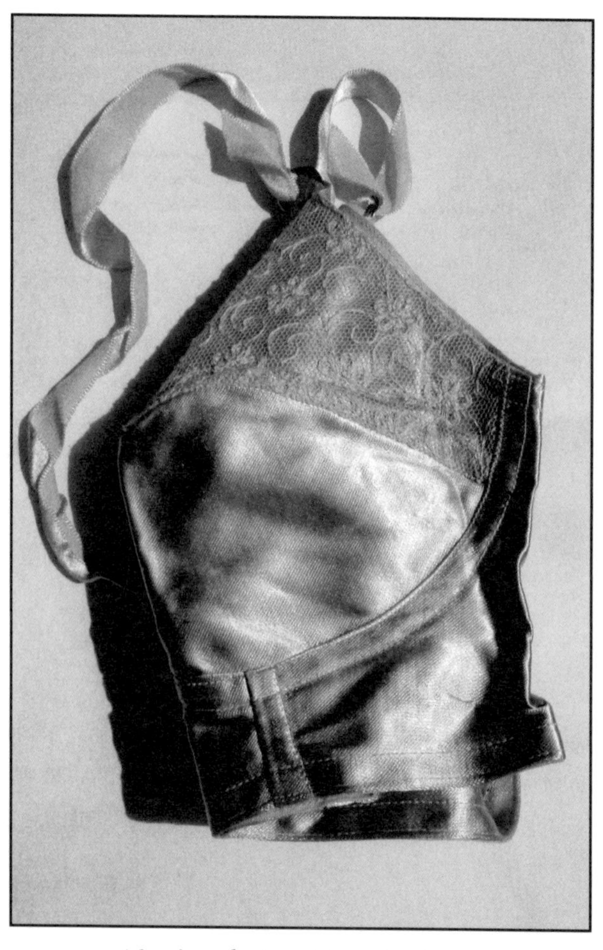

A bra from the Langridge Ltd collection

The Bras and the Bees

Brian peers into the hive; the heavy bee-keeper's hat he's wearing slips forward so that the veil lies flat against the back of his neck. Almost at once a bee takes advantage of the accessible skin and stings him. A sharp needle in the back of the neck, that strange spreading numbness he's so familiar with now.

That night at dinner with Pat, the idea is already half formed.

'What's the use of beekeeping clothing if it doesn't protect you from bees?' he says. 'It's silly getting stung. We could do better.'

And later that week at the factory, Pat gathers together the materials normally used for making bras: boning, net, poly-cotton. She even snaffles a bolt of fabric intended for swimming costume gussets. She sets about designing an improved bee-keeper's veil.

Brian still has the first hoods that he and Pat made together. Looking at them now, they are reminiscent of something you might see on the mood board for a sci-fi movie. They have a futuristic quality, but also seem to reference an earlier era. When not worn, the hood folds together like a concertina, or like a lady's crinoline from the nineteenth century.

Pat made use of a technique that had been in play since the early days of corsetry: boning. The first prototype used eight bones on either side of the head, creating a lightweight supported structure, which held the fabric away from the face and scalp. The only area for which net was used was the face. The net was attached to the rim of the hood with Velcro.

The first hood was a trifle ungainly. It was difficult to stitch because of the shape and the material was not breathable. The white net, which had been intended for the undercups of a Janet Reger bra, was hard to see through, as it reflected the light. But already it was an improvement on what was on the market. Almost by accident, BJ Sherriff Beekeeping Clothing had been born.

Alterations were made. The white net was replaced with black. The inverted teardrop shape of the veil in front of the face was replaced with an oval. Breathable fabric was used.

The perfected beekeeping hood was entered into a competition at the Royal Cornwall Show, where it won first prize. There was palpable excitement and Brian and Pat understood the reason why. The hood and veil they had developed was not just a good design – it was a completely new design in beekeeping.

The beesuit followed. Brian started to think in terms of a diver within a diving bell. If a diver could go down into the sea and look at the fish without drowning, then surely a bee-keeper could be surrounded by bees and not get stung. He wanted to design a beekeeping suit that was, if not watertight, as thoroughly bee-proof as possible.

A bee sting is about one eighth of an inch long. Pat knew that any beesuit they developed needed to be roomy, to keep potential stings away from the body. She used stretch fabric left over from the order of tracksuits for Australian surf lifeguards. With the inspiration of the diver still in mind, the beesuit was gathered and elasticated at the wrists and ankles. Velcro was used to complement zips 'for extra peace of mind'.

When the garment was finished, Brian put it on and tried it out with the bees straight away. It was successful – so much so that a friend asked him to make one for him too. Then another friend asked for one. Brian realised that if bee-keepers he knew personally were asking for these suits, it was likely that there was a wider demand. He and Pat set about improving the design in order to market it.

A separate hood and suit soon metamorphosed into a complete suit. Brian spent many hours working out how the hood could be unzipped and thrown back, or indeed detached completely for laundering.

Cleanliness is very important in bee-keeping, to avoid the transmission of diseases. A zip running all the way around the neck was too awkward to be of any use. Finally Brian hit upon what he referred to as 'the twin zip system', in which two separate horizontal zips start at the nape of the neck and meet at the front of the throat. This design meant the hood could be unzipped in either direction as much or as little as the wearer required and could be removed completely without any difficulty. For added practicality, zips with large ring pulls were employed, easy to use even when wearing gloves.

Before long, there were more innovations: sleeves with elastic loops to go over the thumb, pockets big enough to hold kindling for the smoker and a special pocket for the hive tool. And for the hood, a new kind of veiling was developed which was so easy to see through you could forget you were wearing it. This was named the 'ClearView' veil.

The first beekeeping garment marketed by BJ Sherriff was called The Commercial, as it was intended for bee farmers everywhere. It consisted of a sleeved top and hood and came down as far as the bottom of the ribs. It was intended to be worn over a boiler suit. In 1970 Brian and Pat placed their first advertisements for The Commercial in *The British Bee Journal* and in *Beecraft*.

The editor of the *The British Bee Journal* suggested that they should exhibit at the National Honey Show at Caxton Hall in London and that's exactly what they did.

The first public showing of the beesuit later that year was a great success. Brian recalls standing behind the stand all day, putting the garment on and taking it off again, to demonstrate its features. On, off, on, off. Brian knew he was on to something.

22

Beginning Again

Brian in his new protective beekeeping clothing

Beginning Again

During the final years of Langridge Ltd, Camborne, Brian and Pat had scarcely dared to hope that the bees, and in particular the protective beekeeping clothing they were developing, would provide a way forward. But by 1978 Brian felt for the first time in years that if he'd had the chance to meet his grandfather again, he'd have been able to hold his head up. Langridge Ltd, Camborne was no more, but from the bones of the old enterprise, Brian and Pat had created something entirely new – and revolutionary.

Brian was ready to try his luck with the international market. He advertised in *Gleanings in Bee Cultur*e, a magazine now known more simply as *Bee Culture*. His delight at receiving the first order for eight beesuits from Calgary, Canada cannot be underestimated. It was just the beginning, but it meant everything to Brian.

Expansion was the next step and Brian and Pat were in their element, collaborating as partners in this new business venture. They realised it was essential to get to know their export market and consequently travelled all over the world, meeting bee farmers and bee-keepers from a wide range of backgrounds, and attending conferences. They saw how the working lives of bee-keepers varied dramatically across the globe, due to local circumstances such as climate, indigenous bee species, indigenous flowering plants and many other factors they could never have guessed.

Brian went to see bees in Hawaii and attended conventions in the USA and Canada. In Egypt he learnt that the flat roofs of the houses there make an ideal location for beehives. On one roof he saw a hundred beehives. There he also saw smokers made of cow dung wrapped in hessian sacking and tied tightly with a cord – they looked like cigars – and he saw venom being collected for use in pharmaceutical products.

With Pat, Brian travelled to New Zealand and Australia. In New Zealand, he saw bees being moved into the kiwi fruit orchards at night to assist with pollination. He discovered that traditional white beekeeping suits showed up in the moonlight and attracted bees. So, back in Cornwall, Brian and Pat created a khaki beesuit to solve the problem. It turned out to be very popular, even with those who didn't attend to their bees by moonlight.

Brian became interested in the ways in which bees respond to colour. He consulted research studies and carried out his own investigations. What he found was that dark colours, such as black, emerald green and the blue of mechanics' overalls, seem to make bees more aggressive, whereas pale colours have no such effect. And, interestingly, certain shades of red do not seem to attract the attention of bees.

Following on from this research, Brian and Pat brought out protective beekeeping clothing in a range of colours. In particular, the red or 'salsa' beesuit became a favourite with bee-keepers.

Whenever they saw a need for a modification, Brian and Pat went back to the drawing board. For example, The Honey Rustler was created after one man attended a workshop in a wheelchair and found the smock-like Countryman hard to put on. Brian created a new jacket design with a vertical zip at the front of the garment. Many years later he would create modular suits for amputees.

Brian and Pat's sensitivity to the real-life needs of bee-keepers was undeniable and it was not long before their designs gained them an international following. Brian never took success for granted however. He knew how close he had been to losing everything.

23

A Smile for Everyone

Pat and Brian in their early
square-dancing days

A Smile for Everyone

Brian considered himself a fortunate man. He'd been dealt a good hand in life and even when times had been desperate, his best friend and life partner, Pat, had helped him to bounce back. In October 1994, however, Pat was taken from him suddenly and irrevocably.

In the gardens of the British Beekeeping Association at Stoneleigh in Warwickshire, there is a sundial with Pat Sherriff's name on it. At its foot a gold plaque bears the inscription, 'In memory of Pat Sherriff, Designer of the Sherriff Beekeepers Hood. She had a smile for everyone.' A similar inscription is marked on a bench just to one side of the National Coastwatch Institution lookout at Bass Point in Cornwall.

Brian was at home on the day in question and the first he knew of it was when a policeman came to his front door and rang the doorbell. The officer told him that Pat had died of an asthma attack. It was a complete shock. As the policeman and Brian sat over cups of tea, Brian tried to take it in, but it was impossible. From the moment they had met and throughout their 42 years of marriage, Brian and Pat had been as 'two sides of one'.

Speaking more slowly and more carefully than usual, Brian says: 'It took me a long time to get over that.' And then to lighten the mood he adds: 'I had to learn to cook.'

The bee clothing business gave Brian an excuse to start exploring again and the list of countries he visited is extraordinary: Aruba, Austria, Antigua, Australia, Bolivia, Brazil, Belize, Belgium, the Bahamas, Curaçao, Corsica, China, Canada... the list goes on. In the course of his life, Brian has been a visitor in more than fifty-five countries and he has been a witness to many rare beekeeping practices.

As concerns for the world ecology grew and bee numbers were seen to be in decline, Brian's knowledge became ever more precious and he came to occupy a fairly unique position in the bee world, as an expert with a global perspective.

Brian had heard about an organisation called Bees for Development, which helped individuals in developing countries to establish an independent livelihood through beekeeping. In 1996 he became a pioneer on their first beekeeping safari to Tanzania.

Later, Brian started to give talks about his experiences abroad. These were delivered using slides and two projectors side by side, so that a panoramic view was created. It was also possible for him to present 'before' and 'after' shots simultaneously. As well as covering a range of beekeeping topics, the slideshows included titles such as *The Tiger Trail in Central India* and *Otzi the Ice Man – Frozen in the Alps for 5000 Years*. At any one time Brian would have approximately fifteen different talks on offer and used to give one or two talks a month, usually at venues close to home in Cornwall, usually for charity.

A firm favourite was *The Honey Hunters of Nepal*. The subject of this panoramic slide show was the Nepalese Apis laboriosa, or giant mountain honey bee. It's one of the most ferocious bees in the world and makes its home at an altitude of several thousand metres. For centuries, its enormous combs, clearly visible on the cliff face under outcrops of rock, have held an irresistible allure. Those wishing to harvest the honey need to be skilled mountaineers and the daring methods used by the Nepalese honey hunters have become legendary, but the practice has now almost died out.

In 1997, Brian travelled with a small group of bee experts to Nepal to see for himself. He gained an entry permit to the Annapurna Conservation Area on 23 November and began the trek the following morning. It would be ten days before he got to see the giant mountain honey bees.

Brian and the rest of the group hiked through an exceptional landscape. They crossed a river in a dugout canoe. Two men stood at either end of the canoe and propelled it along by means of long sticks. They passed through the natural habitat of elephants and rhinos and saw oxen at work in the fields. They stayed at the eco-friendly campsite of Ghalekharka and from there made their way to a small village.

Brian was welcomed into one house where he met a woman, who sat with her legs stretched out in front of her, her feet resting on the ends of a loom, passing the shuttles back and forth. She was surrounded by six children, a white billy goat and its kid. One of the children told Brian that a sheep was going to be killed that day.

The woman's husband, who had been lounging against the wall, roused himself and showed Brian the hive they kept in the end wall of their house. When he pulled out one panel, the honeycomb was revealed. The bees were Apis cerana, small black bees with whitish bands on the abdomen, a bit smaller than the European honey bee, Apis mellifera. These were not the giant mountain honey bees Brian had come to see, but he was fascinated none the less.

Brian and the others continued on their way, crossing a river on a rickety bamboo bridge with white water tumbling beneath them and finally climbing a narrow mountain path which led to their destination: a grassy plain with a single herder's hut. To Brian's delight, he discovered that the Nepalese guides had gone on ahead and put up tents for the entire party. He arrived to a welcoming scene: a hot curry and informal dancing.

A dance display was taking place involving just two dancers, a man and a woman. It was chilly and the female dancer was almost entirely covered up with woollen scarves and a sizeable buttoned-up cardigan. The male dancer was wearing jeans, a windcheater and a baseball cap. But as soon as they started to dance, Brian was enthralled. They told stories with their movements, forming their hands skillfully into *mudras* in the traditional style.

Brian woke up to tea, breakfast and a view of the blue-white Annapurna mountain range rising up above their camp, some 8,000 metres above sea level. Below him, he could see the brown terraces of farmland. Finally, after another half day's walk, he reached the home of the giant mountain honey bees.

High up on the scarp cliff face, their combs could clearly be seen. It was hard to judge from a distance, but Brian knew that each comb could be as much as two metres in diameter. He could see thirty-six pale yellow semi-circles, with no camouflage at all against the dark cliff face. Some men had evidently gone on ahead, as there was a rope ladder and additional ropes dangling from the top of the cliff. A guide told Brian and the other visitors that the rope ladder was almost 100 metres long and made of woven bamboo.

As they waited for the hunt to begin, Brian heard about the fate of the sheep. It had indeed been slaughtered. He was told that it was traditional to butcher a sheep or goat and inspect its liver just before a hunt. If the liver looked healthy, it was considered auspicious to proceed. If not, the honey hunt was called off. On this occasion, the hunt was going ahead.

Fires were already being lit at the foot of the cliff. The smoke was rising up the mountainside and the bees, which were grouped in protective formation over the entire surface of each comb, began to rise up, leaving the combs exposed. The honey hunter started to climb, his face covered only by a thin layer of cloth.

The tools for the hunt were laid out on the ground: two bamboo poles, approximately five metres in length. One ended in a fork and the other in a curved blade, rather like a scythe, although sharpened on the outside not the inside edge. Men and women squatted or sat on rocks at the foot of the cliff, the women snugly wrapped in shawls, their heads covered. Brian noticed that most of the women wore traditional clothing with decorated woollen shawls – like the one he had seen being woven – in white, red, mauve and burnt orange. The men wore mostly Western clothing.

Brian and the other visitors stood to watch the proceedings. Each of them had been honoured with a garland of marigolds around the neck and a mark of tikka on their foreheads. Watching as the man climbed the swaying rope ladder raised a single question in Brian's mind: was the sweetness of honey worth risking a man's life for?

The danger involved was evident. Anyone robbing the honeycomb of the giant mountain honey bees would certainly be stung, and those stings could claim a person's life if he or she hadn't developed sufficient immunity. As if that wasn't enough, a fall could be just as perilous.

The honey hunter drew level with the first comb. He sat down on one rung of the ladder and tied himself in place with a cord around the waist. He was ready to begin. First, the forked pole was raised up to him. He used it to pass a piece of cord through the lower section of the comb, where the brood was. Next, the forked pole was lowered and exchanged for the pole with the curved blade. The honey hunter cut the comb from left to right, detaching the brood section, which was lowered down the cliff face on the cord. This protein-rich food would be eaten later.

Next, a basket was conveyed down to the honey hunter from the top of the cliff. He manoeuvred it into position under the honeycomb and steadied it with his foot. He then proceeded to cut tranches of honeycomb, filling the basket and leaving just a narrow strip for the bees to cluster on. The basket was lowered to the ground. This procedure was repeated many times, but six combs were left untouched. The Nepalese guides explained that this was so that the bees would return again the following season to establish new colonies.

The honey hunter began his descent. Almost every part of his face and torso was covered in bees. The basket was lowered for the last time to women waiting at the bottom of the cliff face, who cut the honeycomb into pieces. Most of the honeycomb and wax would be kept for local use and to sell, but the women offered each of the foreign guests, including Brian, a little taste of hard-won honey.

24

The Watchkeeper

Brian Sherriff
in the cutting room at BJ Sherriff

The Watchkeeper

Brian's father was usually to be seen with a cigarette in his mouth, and yet he lived to 96 years of age. Even as an elderly man, he still had the toothbrush moustache he'd had on his wedding day, although it had turned white. When Brian's mother died, Jack was somewhat lost. He started to attend the Christian Spiritualist Church in Falmouth and it was here that he met his second wife, Ethel. They moved into a small flat adjoining her daughter's house in St Merryn, near Padstow, in North Cornwall.

One day Jack said to Brian: 'I want to have my last drive. Could you bring me back?'

So Brian got into his father's Vauxhall and kept his father company while Jack drove for about half a mile. He stopped the car at a junction, they changed seats and Brian drove back. That was Jack's last drive. Jack lived for many more years after that, but he never drove again.

Brian did not remarry. Instead, he considered what he could do with his life that would make a difference. It was three years before he found his new vocation, and when he did, it turned out to be an inspired choice, one which brought together many of the different strands that had run through his life.

Back in the early 1960s, as a young father of two, Brian had bought a holiday bungalow on the Cornish coast, in a conscious or unconscious echo of his parents' lives. The bungalow was situated on the Lizard at Bass Point, the southernmost point in Britain. It was a wild place, desolate at times, with waves crashing onto the granite rocks. But it had appealed to Brian. At the foot of the garden was a Coastguard station and perhaps for Brian this had been the real draw. He remembered that his parents' bungalow on Trevose Head had been built around the wooden remains of an old Coastguard lookout.

Brian had sold his bungalow in 1973, one of the many economies made when the bra business was failing, but his connection to the place had remained as strong as ever. When a national policy decision was made in 1994 to abandon all the

Coastguard stations around the United Kingdom, he was aware of it and shared in the widespread dismay. In this atmosphere of general unease, a tragedy not far from Bass Point focused everyone's minds. Two men set off from Cadgwith on a fishing expedition from which they never returned. There were some who felt that if the Bass Point Coastguard station had been manned, the tragedy could have been avoided. Others said the boat was already too far out when it got into trouble and would not have been seen. In any case, one thing was clear: without a lookout more lives would be lost – and nobody wanted that.

Captain Anthony Starling-Lark responded by setting up the National Coastwatch Institution (NCI). Bass Point was established as the first lookout in operation.

Three years later Brian joined the team as a volunteer watchkeeper. He was a perfect candidate because of his early RAF training as a radio telephone operator. He was given a warm welcome and received a uniform with a star and a single bar on the shoulder. It was May 1997. He was to be a watchkeeper for the next seventeen years.

Brian parked at the Housel Bay Hotel and got out of his car. It was still dark. He carried a torch with him for that reason, but he didn't always switch it on. He liked to see the gradual rising of colour off the sea. To reach the NCI lookout, he had to walk along a short stretch of the coastal path. It was a walk he loved, with the sea to his right, never completely still, always restless, and the silhouette of the lookout to guide him.

He knew that when he walked back to the car in a few hours' time the landscape would be transformed. He'd be able to see the grassy plain, the gorse bushes, the rabbits that occasionally darted across. There would be birds too, tiny songbirds calling back and forth, and rooks, which seemed to be everywhere on the headland, keeping watch – just like him.

At the lookout building he punched in the code and opened the door. As he went inside, he glanced at the noticeboard with its photographs of celebrated sailing ships which had come to grief: Bay of Panama, Adolf Vinnen, Cromdale, as well as more recent newspaper cuttings. It was to avoid this kind of tragedy that he was there.

He walked up the stairs and into the operations room. Before he made coffee, he called the Falmouth Coastguard on the dedicated telephone line.

'Good morning,' he said. 'This is Bass Point lookout. Our watch is now open.'

The NCI lookout at Bass Point is a narrow two-storey building, with a balcony around the outside, situated just in front of the original Coastguard station. The Red Ensign and NCI flag fly from a mast at the side of the lookout. The aim of the NCI is to provide a listening and visual watch along the British coastline during daylight hours. Over the years, volunteer watchkeepers have helped hundreds of vessels in trouble, not to mention sub-aqua divers, rock-climbers, walkers and surfers. Potential emergencies include shipwrecks, strandings, fires at sea, collisions, man overboard situations – in fact any accidents happening on land, in the air or at sea in the vicinity.

NCI watchkeepers have come to be viewed as a vital part of the UK Search and Rescue network, and are now recognised by Her Majesty's Coastguard, but this was not always the case. Brian remembers that in the early days when he made his call to the Falmouth Coastguard each morning, they did not seem remotely interested.

Every Saturday Brian made his way to the lookout to carry out his watch. Sometimes, when the winds were very strong, it was impossible to approach the lookout from the coastal path. Watchkeepers had been known to be literally blown off their feet. On such days, Brian took a diversion through what had once been his own garden. There were two stones missing in the garden wall and the new owners had given him permission to climb across the gap.

The equipment at the lookout was minimal at first – just a telephone, a pair of binoculars and two log-books. In one, Brian recorded all the vessels that passed within eight miles of the shore, noting the direction of travel and the distance. In the other, he recorded everything that happened on land. On a foggy day, it was sometimes impossible to know what was out there. Brian and the other volunteers found that they were straining their eyes through a telescope to read the name on a vessel. They relied heavily on chart work.

It did not take Brian long to apply his mind to the question of how funds could be raised for Bass Point. His solution was, not surprisingly, to give a series of panoramic slide shows with titles such as *Shipwrecks Around The Lizard, Shipwrecks Around the Isles of Scilly* and *Wreck and Rescue from the Lizard to Land's End*. For these he charged an entrance fee. Brian raised more than £3,000 for the NCI at Bass Point and it was partly due to his efforts that they were able to acquire new technologies: ship-to-shore radio, AIS and radar.

After ten years of service, Brian received a second bar on his uniform in recognition of his work. He continued as a watchkeeper for a further seven years, until an accident intervened. He was out walking one day on a different headland when he broke his fifth metatarsal. He bravely carried on with his walk and even drove home using his injured foot to operate the clutch on his car. It was Friday. At home the foot began to swell and by the end of the weekend it was so huge that shoes were out of the question. His daughter Angela found him in socks and sandals on Monday morning and drove him straight to Accident and Emergency. Watches at the NCI were now uncomfortable for Brian with a foot that was causing him pain. He decided that at 86 years of age, after 584 watches, it might be time for him to stop.

Brian's resignation was accepted gracefully, but his colleagues at the NCI had no intention of letting him go that easily. His name appeared on the rota the following year. He had not been put down for any watches; he was simply given the title 'fund-raiser'.

The sense of adventure, which prompted Brian to teach himself square dancing from a book, travel the world and start a new business from scratch when times were hard, has not deserted him and it is likely it never will. In recent years, Brian has worked as a volunteer at a wide variety of organisations including the RNLI in Falmouth, Lanhydrock House – a late-Victorian stately home where he was in charge of the children's room and doll's house – St Michael's Mount and Chysauster ancient village near Penzance. At Chysauster, Brian's job was to show people around the ruins of some late Iron Age stone hut circles. There are many mysteries surrounding the place and when anyone asked a difficult question, Brian reportedly 'made up a good story'.

It's been quite a few years since Brian delivered his series of panoramic slide shows, but recently a local group contacted him asking if he would consider it, as the speaker they had booked cancelled at short notice. Brian, at 89, thought nothing of dusting off his slides for *Shipwrecks Around the Lizard*. On the appointed day, as he took up position behind twin projectors, it was clear he had something special to offer. He looked around the room with his bright blue eyes. There was an openness and a directness to his gaze – and the dancing likelihood of humour. It is rare to meet a man so open to life and so fearless.

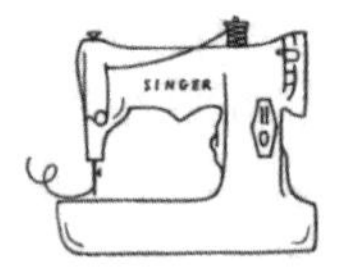
SINGER

The BJ Sherriff Legacy

The Bra-kerchief in its presentation pack

The BJ Sherriff Legacy

It is fifty years since Pat and Brian sat down together and sketched out their plans for a new kind of beekeeping hood and veil. It was one of those idle back-of-an-envelope moments, but Pat's design answered a real need in beekeeping and transformed protective clothing for bee-keepers across the world.

Today BJ Sherriff Beekeeping Clothing and Equipment, with Brian's daughter Angela at the helm, is recognised world-wide. It continues to meet an international demand, as well as making bespoke garments on request, such as modular suits for amputees. All garments are made in Cornwall and, whenever possible, locally sourced materials are used.

Brian continues to travel to exotic locations and loves to meet bee-keepers in all walks of life, but he also derives great pleasure from driving out to his sewing-machinists every week to deliver cut work and collect finished garments, and he still takes special orders to the post office in person.

In order to bring together the many people who care about bees in the UK, Brian and Angela set up the BEE Fayre at Enys House and Gardens in Penryn, a beautiful Cornish stately home famous for its bluebell woods. The Fayre runs over one or two days in August, with talks, workshops, demonstrations and experienced bee-keepers on hand to answer questions.

Acknowledgements

This work is a book of memoir that reflects the honest recollections of Brian Sherriff, but some names, characteristics and locales may have been changed and dialogue added. Notebooks provided by Brian Sherriff were used to recreate scenes from his life.

The author and publisher gratefully acknowledge the permission granted to reproduce copyright material. The quotation from the play *Still Life* by Noel Coward, first published in 1936, has been included with the permission of Methuen. The chapter title *Music While You Work* has been included with the permission of the BBC. The photograph of Brian Sherriff and Patricia Harvey at the Assembly Ball in Bath, taken by Bert Hardy in 1952, has been included with the permission of Getty Images. Every effort has been made to trace copyright holders and to obtain their permission for the use of copyright material. The author and publisher apologise for any errors or omissions in the above list and would be grateful if notified of any corrections.

Firstly, I would like to thank Angela Sherriff for inviting me to write this book, and Brian Sherriff for agreeing to meet with me over a period of a year as the manuscript was taking shape. It has been a great privilege and a profound pleasure to spend time with Brian.

Thank you to everyone at BJ Sherriff for the friendly welcome I received, cups of tea and help with research. My thanks go to Clare Bourne, Jo Field, Bev Smith, Lianne Heyward, Sandra Vincent and all at BJ Sherriff headquarters.

I acknowledge with gratitude the following individuals and organisations, who helped me with my research for this book: Bristol Archives; Bristol Central Library; Cornish Studies Library; The Cornubia, Temple Street, Bristol; Phil Draper of the website Church Crawler; Professor Juliet Osborne and Professor Natalie Hempel de Ibarra, the University of Exeter; Peter W Jones, International Bomber Command Archive, The University of Lincoln; Mike Kipling for sharing the results of his research on The Langridges and the Gibbons; Dr CS

Knighton, Principal Assistant Keeper of Archives, Clifton College; Helen McArdle, historical costumier; Andy Price at the King's Head, Victoria Street, Bristol; Kevin Wilkinson, Ancestry Hunter (theancestry-hunter.com); Jean Wills (née Tenby) and Sandra Vincent, former employees of Langridge Ltd, Camborne; Steve Wood and Alan Bryant of Kingswood Heritage Museum; Judith Wright, senior archivist at The Boots Archive.

I would also like to thank: Faisel Baig, Gillian Doherty, Wendy Edwards, Alexandra Gibbons, Theo Jones, Sarita Mohapatra, Sambit Mohapatra, Ann, Garth, Frederica and Paul Notley, Simon Parker, Kristien Potgieter, Dominic Power, Sarelle Reid, Alan Robinson, The Religious Society of Friends (Quakers), Rashmee Roshan Lall, Emma Timpany and Marcus Williamson.

FA Notley

Chapter Notes

P5. Photograph of Patricia Harvey and Brian Sherriff. Hardy, B (1952). Picture Post (Vol 55 No 11), pp.20-21. Reprinted with permission. The caption in *Picture Post* accompanying this photograph read: 'Moment in History. It's one o'clock. The night air is caressingly warm, the Roman stone impossibly cold against her shoulders. The alcove is two thousand years old; the story is much older than that.'

Chapter 2: The Beginning

P23. 'The bride was given away by her father...'. Unidentified source.

P25. Welby, W. (1934). Naked and Unashamed: Nudism from Six Points of View. London: Thorsons.

P26. 'She is reading a Boots library book...' The quotation is taken from the play *Still Life* which forms part of the collection *Tonight at 8.30* by Noel Coward, first published in 1936. Used with permission. Copyright resides with Methuen. Information about Boots Libraries kindly provided by Boots Archive.

Chapter 4: The Gentleman Bicyclist

P38. Portrait of EJ Sherriff. Initialled AFB. EJ Sheriff, Sydenham B. C. [Etching] (n.d.) Bicycling News.
P41. Extracts taken from Bicycling News, Sherriff, E (1879-1880).
P45. 'A very useful man at cricket, hockey and tennis' Unidentified source.
P46. United Kingdom Census, 1891.
P47. Letter to Bertha Sherriff from Edgar Sherriff, undated.
P49. Letter to Bertha Sherriff from Kay Montgomery, née Sherriff, undated.
P50. United Kingdom Census, 1901.

Chapter 5: Raising the Dust

P54. Langridge, Richard, Stay and Corset Maker, Wholesale and Retail: 63 Castle Street, Matthew's Annual Bristol Directory, 1816, p.98.
P54. Another address associated with Langridge's stay factory is Avon Cliff House, Totterdown, Bristol. This seems to have been George Langridge's residence but was also referred to in an advertisement for 'The Symmetrically Formed Paris Corset'. The Totterdown site is mentioned in Willmott, J. (2004). Kingswood and Two Mile Hill. Stroud: Tempus.

P57. History of Temple Church. Available at: english-heritage.org.uk.
P59. The Langridges and the Gibbons. Available at: genealogy.kipling.me.uk.
P59. 'Awfully sudden death…' Bristol Mercury, 20 September 1815.
P60. 'A moiety of the Premises...' Bristol Mercury, 3 April 1886.

Chapter 7: On the Other Side of the Curtain

P73. Sherriff, D. The Temple of the Sacred Heart. Camborne, Cornwall.

Chapter 8: Music While You Work

P77. Music While You Work (1940). (Radio programme) BBC. With permission.
P80. Further information about Langridge (Kingswood) Ltd can be found at the Kingswood Heritage Museum, Bristol and in Willmott, J. (2004). Kingswood and Two Mile Hill. Stroud: Tempus.
P85. London Zoo during World War Two. Available at: zsl.org.
P85. Bristol During World War Two. Available at: humanities.uwe.ac.uk.

Chapter 11: The Inheritance

I am indebted to Helen McArdle, historical

costumier, for assistance with this chapter and to Wendy Edwards for modelling the corset.
P117. "radium, n." OED online.

Chapter 12: The Reluctant Apprentice
P123. 'If you are going to be a saleswoman...' Bacon, E. The Foundationwear Fitter's Handbook. London: The Corset Guild of Great Britain.

Chapter 14: A Wanderlust
P153. Hunt, R. H/Q Civil Liaison, Land Kaernten, British Troops in Austria I. 14 August 1950. Letter to Brian Sherriff.
P154. J Thomann's Nachfolger. 16 September 1950. Letter to Brian Sherriff.

Chapter 16: Sheriff Bryan and his Square Dance Posse
P171. 'sheriff, n.' OED Online.
P172. In 1788 Aylesbury County Gaol was situated between County Hall and Walton Street. The gaol later moved to its current site on Bierton Road where it became HM Prison.
P174. Bath and Wilts Chronicle and Herald, 18 June 1952.

Chapter 17: Featherwhite
P180. Lewin's Mead Meeting, Bristol. 2 December 1953. Letter to Brian and Pat Sherriff.

Chapter 18: The Bra-kerchief
P186. An Introduction to Your Work with Langridge Ltd. (1961). Camborne: The Camborne Printing & Stationery Co Ltd.
P192. There were many dignitaries present at the official opening of the factory at Vean Road, including the Mayor of Camborne. Brian remembers that Sam Wilson, clerk to the council, was there, a man who had worked hard to get industry into the area. Wilson Way in Pool still bears his name.

Chapter 19: Twelve Stitches per Inch
P197. 'Girls at Langridge's...' The West Briton and Royal Cornwall Gazette, 30 September 1965. Our Girls Get Good Pay, Says Firm with Bulging Order Book. p.13.

Chapter 20: Fighting for Survival
P209. For his knowledge about the technique of 'bleeding', Brian acknowledges this source: Whitcombe, H. (1956). Bees

are my business. Gollancz.
P210. 'Firm Fights for Survival', Bennetts, B. The West Briton, 14 January 1971. p.1.

Look After The Bees

Brian supports a wide range of bee charities and initiatives in Britain and overseas, as does the company he founded, BJ Sherriff Protective Clothing for Bee-keepers.

Bees Abroad

Brian is a patron of Bees Abroad, an organisation which uses bee-farming as a way to help people in developing countries gain financial independence. The charity aims to help the poorest in society by providing training and education in everything related to bees. Initiatives make use of indigenous bees, local materials and local beekeeping practices.

The Bee Farmers Association Apprenticeship

BJ Sherriff is a sponsor of the Bee-a-Bee Farmer Apprenticeship scheme. Run in association with Rowse Honey, this scheme accepts applications from 16 to 24 year-olds wishing to undergo a three-year training apprenticeship, which leads to a diploma recognised by the Worshipful Company of Wax Chandlers. The apprentices are paid – the scheme is part-funded by the British government – and they are each presented with a complimentary white monogrammed BJ Sherriff beesuit. They complete courses in practical skills including queen bee rearing and stock improvement, botany and forage sources, pollen and nutrition, processing hive products, bottling and presentation, carpentry and woodworking and, crucially, marketing, finance and setting up a business.

Bees for Development

Bees for Development assists individuals in developing countries, with a particular emphasis on women and young people, helping them to establish independent, resilient livelihoods by means of beekeeping. Brian has visited a number of Bees for Development projects over the years, having been a pioneer on their first Beekeeping Safari to Tanzania in 1996. Brian continues to raise funds for Bees for Development and BJ Sherriff provides beautiful hampers for their bee-themed fundraising events.

The Bee Kind Appeal

The Bee Kind Appeal was launched by Cornwall Wildlife Trust with the aim of protecting wild bees by creating and preserving their natural habitat. It has a particular focus on bee species local to Cornwall, including the tormentil mining bee, the long-horned bee, the green-eyed flower bee, the moss carder bee and the brown-banded carder bee.

Eat Natural

Eat Natural makes cereal bars in the UK. In 2016 the company launched an initiative called Pollenation, with an emphasis on celebrating bees nationally. At the centre of its vision is the desire to reverse the decline of bees in Great Britain. Eat Natural commissioned the design of sustainable beehives made from disused wooden pallets, a by-product of their own food production. Each of these is fitted with an Arnia hive-monitoring system which records the temperature, weight, sound, humidity, bee count and queen status of a hive. The information supplied through the monitoring system is sent directly to the bee-keeper and is also collated for research. There is an alert to let a bee-keeper know if a hive has been rustled. As part of the initiative, twenty-five new bee-keepers, of all age-groups and from diverse backgrounds, are given training and equipment each year, to encourage a renaissance of British beekeeping.

The Good Life Project and Bees for Business

BJ Sherriff is a sponsor of The Good Life Project, which carries out research into the effects of activities allied to the natural world to establish whether these are demonstrably beneficial to human health and wellbeing. The Good Life Project set up Bees for Business, a novel incentive by which individuals and corporations can rent, adopt or buy beehives.

Help for Heroes

Help for Heroes offer courses in bee-keeping to wounded, injured and sick veterans, service personnel and their families. The courses cover a range of topics including the history of the honey bee, equipment requirements, managing common diseases and harvesting honey. BJ Sherriff has donated beekeeping suits to Help for Heroes and have also developed modular suits for amputees.

Pengam Hives

Pengam Hives is a not for profit charitable organisation which runs an apiary in Pengam, South Wales. BJ Sherriff has supported them with the donation of beesuits.

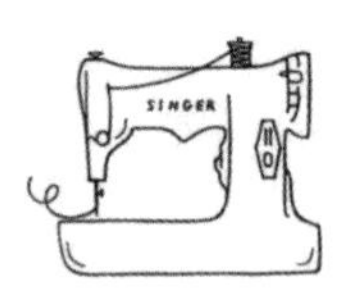
SINGER

SINGER

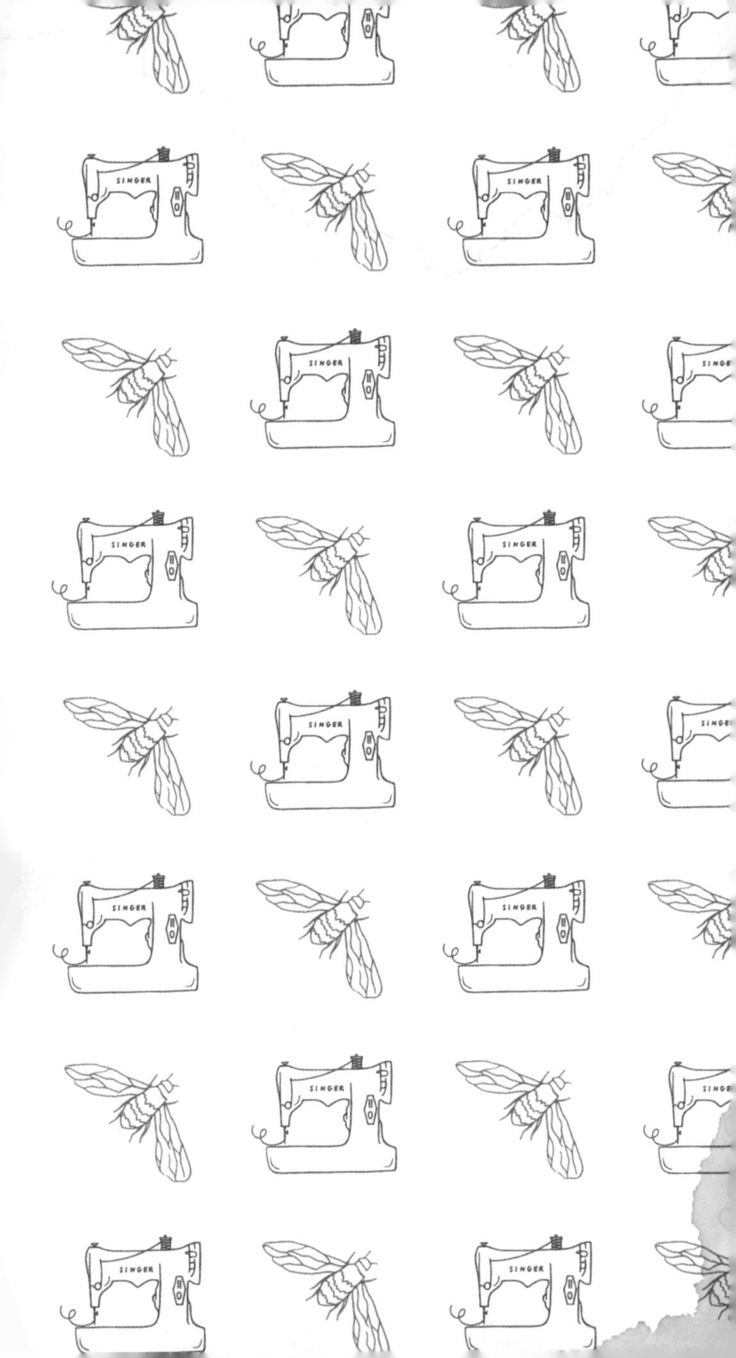
SINGER

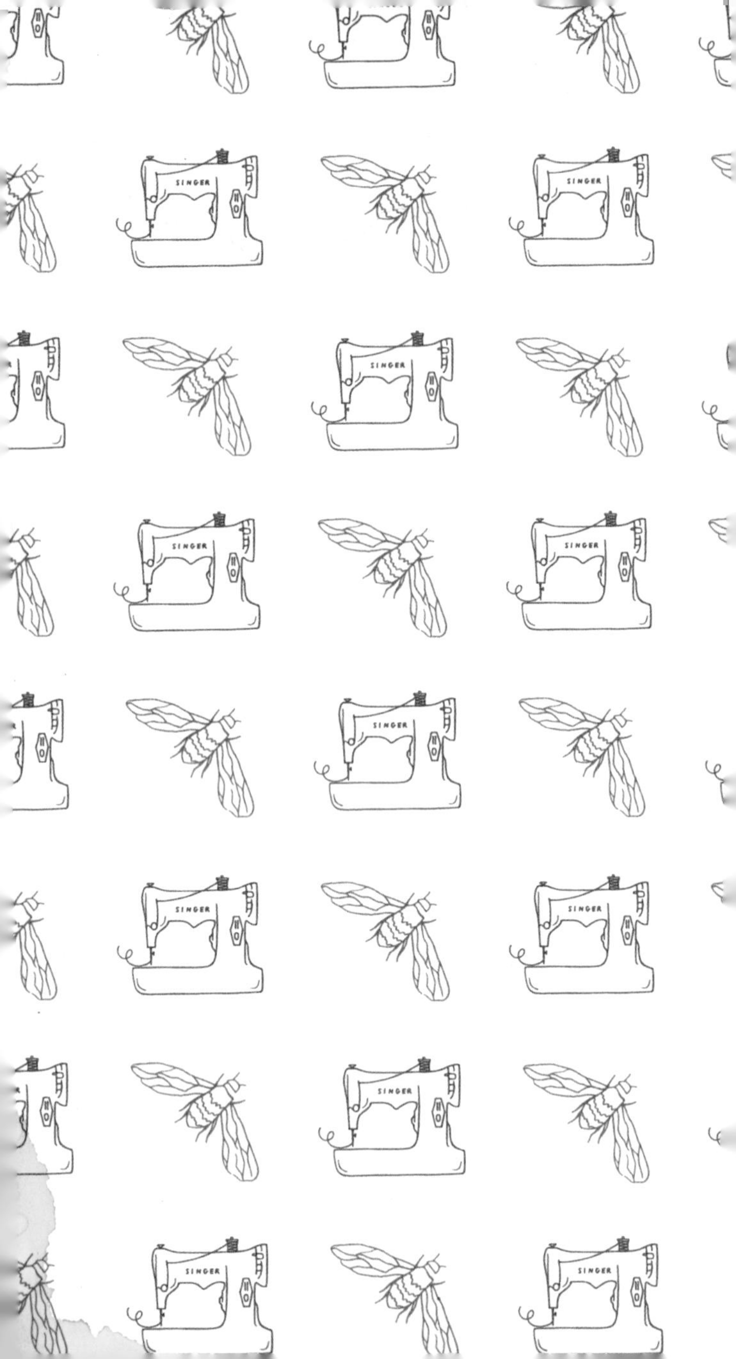
SINGER